Table of Contents

Objectives..	5
What is a ProDoula Postpartum & Infant Care Doula...................	7
Vulnerability...	10
The ProDoula Philosophy..	10
DISC...	12
DISC Matrix..	13
Always Provide Non-Judgmental Support.....................................	18
Listening Styles...	19
Understanding the Subtext of the Birth Story..............................	21
Postpartum Planning Session...	23
Emotional Adjustment to Parenthood..	25
Social Media and Parenthood...	26
Perinatal Mood & Anxiety Disorders..	28
Edinburgh Postnatal Depression Scale (EPDS).............................	34
The Early Postpartum Period...	38
Physical Recovery From Birth..	40
Postpartum Discharge Instructions..	47
Vaginal Soreness...	49
Vaginal Discharge...	50
Contractions...	50
Postpartum Diaphoresis/Sweating...	50
Urination Problems...	50
Hemorrhoids and Bowel Movements..	51
Cesarean Birth Recovery..	52
Hair Loss and Skin Changes..	53
Weight Loss..	53
The Postpartum Checkup..	53
Postpartum Red Flags...	53
Infant Care...	56
Instructions in Newborn Care Basics...	56
Holding and Handling Newborns...	57
Umbilical Cord Care..	57
Diapering..	58
Diaper Rash..	59
Cloth Diapering..	60
Care of the Intact Penis..	61
Circumcision..	61
Bathing...	62
Taking the Baby's Temperature...	66

Medications..	68
Newborn and Infant Safety..	69
Infant Care Red Flags..	71
Developmental Milestones...	73
Vaccines...	81
Caring for Premature Babies/Medically Fragile Babies..........	81
Multiples..	84
Growth Charts...	88
Navigating What We Don't Know...	90
Obtain a Broad Sense of Knowledge..	90
Common Baby Products...	91
Product Safety Recalls...	92
The Tertiary Focus...	93
Sibling Care...	93
Meal Preparation...	94
Household Support...	96
Parenting Philosophies..	98
Comfort & Soothing..	101
Swaddling..	101
Pacifier Use..	102
Self Soothing...	103
Swinging, Bouncing, and Rocking..	104
Overstimulation..	106
Sleep Shaping..	106
Baby-Directed Sleep...	108
Safe Infant Sleep...	109
Infant Feeding...	113
Establishing Breast or Chest Feeding.......................................	114
The Asymmetric Latch..	114
Bodyfeeding Positions..	115
Determining Adequate Intake..	116
Challenges with Breast or Chest Feeding................................	118
Breast or Chest Feeding Red Flags...	120
Alternative Means of Milk Transfer...	122
Expression and Storage of Milk..	125
Breast Pumps...	125
Manual Expression..	126
Milk Storage and Warming...	127
Bottle Feeding...	129
Paced Bottle Feeding..	131

Burping a Baby	133
Reflux	135
Formula Feeding	136
The Ever-Evolving Role of the Postpartum & Infant Care Doula	139
Entry Level Business for Doulas	140
What Doula Business Model is Right for You?	141
Decide on Pricing	142
Insurance Coverage/Reimbursement	143
A Website	143
Get Doula Insurance	145
Create Contracts	146
Business Forms	150
Marketing Your Doula Business	151
Streams of Income for Your Doula Business	153
Growing Your Doula Business	154
The Two Ways We Get Hired	155
The Interview	155
Goal Setting	158

Objectives

Congratulations on taking the first step toward becoming a professional Postpartum and Infant Care Doula! We are honored that you have chosen ProDoula as your training and certification organization and we look forward to supporting you every step of the way.

This comprehensive Postpartum and Infant Care Doula training will provide you with the necessary skills to support future clients as they transition away from pregnancy and welcome a new baby into their family. This standardized curriculum, as well as the inspired dialogue that accompanies it, will deepen your understanding of parenting philosophies and how they impact parent choices, the physical and emotional recovery that happens after birth, evidence-based infant care, including infant feeding support, and so much more. You will learn how to support clients - physically, educationally, and emotionally - and build their confidence during the postpartum period.

One of ProDoula's founding principles is professional, non-judgmental support. Therefore, this training will equip you with the necessary skills to support clients based on the parenting philosophies that are authentic to them. As a ProDoula doula, you will learn how to leave your biases about birth and the postpartum period at the door so that you can provide your clients with the true non-judgmental support that they hire you for.

This postpartum doula training provides you with an opportunity to process your thoughts and experiences regarding the initial postpartum period. It is essential that you do not intentionally or unintentionally impact your clients' experiences negatively; this is why it is important to process these things in your training rather than while you are supporting others. During this course, you will learn about DISC, a personality assessment tool that pertains to improved communication. By better understanding how individuals communicate and process information, you will learn to attune to the clients you serve by supporting them based on their individual communication preferences.

Your knowledge of DISC will also assist you in attracting and signing clients. You may even enhance some existing personal relationships with this newly learned skill.

You will be given step-by-step instructions on how to complete your certification following this training. ProDoula values certification and encourages you to complete this process. Remember, the comprehensive certification exam is part of your training and by doing the research needed to complete this exam you will broaden and build on your own skills and knowledge.

And finally, this Postpartum and Infant Care Doula training will delve into the specifics needed to establish and run a doula business, build a successful brand, and attract your target clients. ProDoula firmly believes in elevating the doula profession from unpaid hobby to successful career, and this course seeks to give you the basic business know-how to do just that.

Following this Postpartum and Infant Care Doula training, the doula will be able to:

- Provide physical, educational, and emotional support to clients seeking postpartum doula support.
- Demonstrate a comprehensive understanding of basic newborn care, support clients using various infant feeding methods, assist clients with their postpartum recovery, become familiar with postpartum mood and anxiety disorders, and will have the ability to provide exceptional support in each scenario.
- Understand and evaluate each client's personality style and attune to them in order to better support each client and their partner.
- Know the steps needed to establish a legitimate doula business and understand the key tenets of how to run a successful business that attracts clients.
- Follow the steps needed to become a ProDoula Certified Postpartum & Infant Care Doula.

What is a ProDoula Postpartum & Infant Care Doula?

The ProDoula Postpartum & Infant Care Doula (P&ICD) brings experience, companionship, and emotional support to parents and their newborns while providing physical, educational, and non-judgmental support. The P&ICD plays an important role in the new family's adjustment to parenthood by being physically present, emotionally available, and fully equipped with the most current evidence-based information surrounding postpartum recovery and newly born babies.

The ProDoula Postpartum & Infant Care Doula's primary, secondary, and tertiary focus are:

Primary Focus:
The physical and emotional recovery of the birthing person

Secondary Focus:
The newborn's transition to life on the outside of the womb

Tertiary Focus:
To help with anything that gets in the way of the primary or secondary focus

The doula has a comprehensive understanding of the normal physical and emotional needs of the postpartum client. Additionally the doula is trained to recognize the early signs and symptoms of anything beyond the scope of normal and refers to the client's medical provider in these instances.

The doula is well versed in infant feeding, sleep support, infant soothing, and general coping skills to help the new parents understand their baby and build their confidence.

Lastly, the doula provides light household support by handling the day to day tasks that may inhibit the client's physical and emotional recovery and/or their ability to bond with their baby. This includes meal preparation, light housework, or other general needs of the family during the postpartum period and beyond.

There are a few things that a doula is not. The doula does not act as a nurse or caregiver and does not provide clinical or medical care to the client, such as physical examinations, assessments, or client/baby monitoring. The doula does not make medical or philosophical decisions for the parents or speak to medical providers on the client's behalf. The doula can help the parents better understand scenarios, provide information for decision-making, and prepare them with the proper language to best communicate their choices. The doula works for the parents and simultaneously maintains a cohesive relationship with their caregivers at all times.

The ProDoula philosophy of providing unbiased, evidence-based support that enables the stability and empowerment of families begins with doulas that are professional and educated, as well as nurturing and compassionate. This manual and the training that accompanies it will equip you with the education necessary to support postpartum families as they settle into their new "normal" after giving birth. Upon completion of your training, you will have the ability to hold space for your client's new and evolving emotions, while validating and affirming the feelings that accompany this vulnerable period of time. Your responsibility is to come to each client with the judgment-free approach that enables them to make the choices that are best for them.

It is essential that you become well versed in the following three foundational doula skills:

1. Connection/Attunement: By understanding a variety of personality styles, and learning how to communicate best with each, you will find that it is not difficult to connect with your clients and create a space where they are able to feel deeply connected to you.
2. Non-judgmental Support: By knowing how to truly free yourself from judgment and bias, and offering the level of support that comes with it, your clients will feel safe and supported in your presence as they find their own path through early parenthood and beyond.
3. Active Listening: By perfecting your skills as an active listener, your clients will feel affirmed, validated, and understood as they process their own fear, worry, and/or anxiety during the postpartum period.

As a ProDoula Postpartum & Infant Care Doula, you are uniquely positioned and have the ability to improve your community by shining a light on the true value of postpartum doula support. Postpartum doulas enable the empowerment of new parents and help build their confidence. Sure, some bottles might get washed or a load of baby laundry folded here and there, but the REAL work is so much deeper than that.

It is crucial that you understand the postpartum doula's role, not just for the clients you serve, but also so you can educate your community about this vital service. Proper education will go hand in hand with selling postpartum support, thus allowing you to raise awareness and establish a financially viable career for yourself.

The ProDoula team is on its own journey to support and enable the empowerment of others through our people and our programs and we want to thank you for joining us on this journey.

Vulnerability

Vulnerability is defined as the "quality or state of being exposed to the possibility of being attacked or harmed, either physically or emotionally." (Source: Oxford English Dictionary) The early postpartum period is a time of extreme emotional vulnerability for many new parents. They often grapple with the fear of being judged by others, the fear of potential errors when caring for their new baby, the fear that they are not "good enough" parents, a limiting belief in their abilities, and so much more. It requires a great deal of trust to allow a new person into their space during this time. However, this is exactly what our clients do. Our clients trust us not only with the care of their new baby, but with their emotional vulnerability as well.

When supporting a client during such a vulnerable time, one must focus on building a personal connection between themselves and the client. Actively listening while maintaining a willingness to be authentic and honest is foundational in mastering attunement and providing non-judgmental support.

The doula must listen and respond, hold space without judgment, and compassionately attune as the client's emotions present themselves in real time. These genuine exchanges enable deep connection and create a safe space for the client to share authentically and receive the support they need and desire.

The ProDoula Philosophy

The ProDoula philosophy is based on the desire to elevate the role of doulas to a professional level in the eyes of expectant individuals and partners, medical professionals, and doulas themselves.

We do this by:

Defying the Doula Stereotype

The word doula represents a profession, NOT a philosophy.

Unfortunately, a stereotype has been created by others that may impact you in some way. These stereotypes can mislead potential clients to think that you will look and behave a certain way and have a bias toward a more "natural" approach to birth and parenting. A potential client that is more "mainstream" may be anxious about hiring a doula because of those stereotypes. You can help change these concerns for families by being unbiased and professional in all of your interactions as a doula.

DISC

The Personality Assessment

DISC is a personality assessment tool based on the theories of American psychologist William Marston. The theory centers around four different personality traits: Dominant, Influential, Security Minded, and Compliant.

Dominant – Desire for power, control, and authority

Influential – Desire for social interaction, constant communication, praise, and recognition

Security Minded – Is patient, persistent, and thoughtful; seeks the same in return

Compliant – Requires structure and organization

DISC Matrix

D	I	S	C
Dominant Driven Demanding Determined Decisive Delegates	Inspirational Influencing Inducing Impressive Interactive Interested in people	Supportive Submissive Stable Steady Sentimental Shy	Cautious Competent' Calculating Concerned Careful Contemplative

Characteristics

D	I	S	C
Result oriented Quick decisions Need for control Power/authority Makes own rules	People oriented Loves to talk Motivational Enthusiastic Recognition oriented	Family oriented Loyal Slow to change Security minded Follows rules	Detail oriented Perfectionist Critical Analytical Takes time to change

Communications

D	I	S	C
Let them talk. They will tell you what they want. They may not listen to you.	Focus on relationship building. Follow their lead. Take an interest in them.	You talk most. May not ask questions. Focus on flexibility. Ask open-ended questions.	Don't get too personal. Answer questions thoroughly. Build credibility.

Benefits Focus

D	I	S	C
You will be in total control. Nothing will happen to you without your permission. Empower them.	I will be with you the whole time. We will do this together. You're going to be amazing.	I will explain everything to you as it's happening. You will feel completely safe.	You will feel as if you have a postpartum expert with you. I will explain everything to you as it is happening. We will cover every detail.

Biggest Root Fear

D	I	S	C
Losing Control	Being judged, alone	The safety of their baby and themselves	Not understanding the process

Close the Interview

D	I	S	C
Be direct. Give them the contract and let them decide what happens next.	Share an excited compliment and express a desire to work with them.	Express your comfort level with them and offer your contract.	Give them the contract and other written information.

Why Is This Important for the Client?

A client who is primarily a **"D"** personality style is used to feeling "in control" and typically holds a position of authority at home and work. They are confident and they easily make quick decisions. They are most uncomfortable when people are "wishy washy" and they prefer to be spoken to respectfully and directly. This person is comfortable expressing what they need and will not hesitate to ask the questions they want answered. They can become frustrated when being given details that are not relevant to them and they are not usually interested in the opinions of others unless they ask.

A client who is primarily an **"I"** personality style seeks strong engaging relationships with others and will likely be excited about making a connection with their doula. "I" personalities love social interaction and are typically enthusiastic and talkative. They are excited to share this period of their life with people who are interested in them and who can be a sounding board to their experience. In many cases, they feel at their best when they are not alone. Making suggestions about doing things that are fun and engaging will appeal to this client and will likely enhance their postpartum experience. This client responds well to praise, recognition, and encouragement, and feels great in the presence of those that offer it.

A client who is primarily an **"S"** personality will likely be security minded and family focused. They are often soft spoken and typically take a cautious approach to new people and new situations. They are most comfortable when things feel safe and predictable. They are a nurturer by nature and can easily forget that you are there to care for them. If not gently reminded, they can quickly slip into caring for you. This individual may also be sentimental. Consider reminding them to save things such as the baby's wristband from the hospital or offer to organize a list of the baby gifts they receive in order to keep track and write personalized thank you notes to each. Be patient and allow this client the time they need to get comfortable. If they feel safe with you, they will want you with them every time they bring a baby home.

A client who is primarily a **"C"** personality thrives on evidence-based information. They are not typically interested in opinions; they prefer facts. They gather information and make decisions based on their findings. They often prefer to follow a well-researched plan and may like to record important information. Suggesting a spreadsheet to track feedings, sleep, wet diapers, and bowel movements may keep them feeling confident and in control.

They are not usually looking to build an instant relationship with the doula. Instead, they seek the knowledge and up-to-date information that the doula can provide.

Once credibility has been established, it is likely that a meaningful relationship will follow.

Supporting the Client

Let's consider the following scenarios. Imagine that it is your client's first day home with their baby. Think about what this time may look like for the parent(s). Did they have a vaginal or cesarean birth? Have they adopted? Had a surrogate? Are they bottle feeding or breastfeeding?

The following scenarios will help you identify behaviors that can help you understand the personality style that your client is presenting in. Remember to take note of the client's personality type and communicate in a language that is comfortable for them.

D	Ask questions like, "What is the most important thing I can do for you today?" Be sure to follow their organization of things.
I	Encourage them to share their birth story with you. Be talkative and personally engaging.
S	Encourage the client to engage your help with household chores or the baby. Remind them that you are not their guest; you are there to support them.
C	Focus on the evidence-based information they are interested in. Ask questions and lead them to current information and recommendations.

It is important to remember that personality styles are fluid. While each individual can exhibit traits from all four styles, most will have two styles that are more dominant. New experiences, stress, and doubt or insecurity may influence which trait is most dominant at any given time. Remember to respond to your client in the style they are presenting.

First Day Scenarios - Consider which personality style is presenting in each scenario

- At your very first shift with your client, you come to the door to find a sign that says: "Please take off your shoes when entering, put on a mask (provided), and wash your hands well before coming to meet parents and baby. Thank you so much!"

- Your client shares with you that they attended a parent and baby meet-up yesterday. When they arrived, everyone was babywearing and breastfeeding. They felt out of place with their baby in the carseat and ready-made bottle of formula at hand so they left immediately.

- When you arrive for your first overnight shift with a client, they tell you, "I've been breastfeeding but my baby hasn't had any wet diapers in 6 hours. They're supposed to have 3 wet ones today, so I'm becoming afraid that I don't have enough milk."

- When you get a moment alone with your client, they say to you: "Thank goodness you're here. I was hoping you could talk with my mother in law about the current safe sleep guidelines because she keeps putting blankets and stuffed animals in the baby's bassinet, and I have to remove them when she's not looking."

- While sitting in the living room with the baby, you overhear your client say to their partner: "Your mom had the audacity to come over today and tell me that I was spoiling our baby by not putting her down to sleep when she was drowsy. Either you have a conversation with her or I will."

- During an emotional conversation with your client, they tearfully say: "I always tell my partner how great they are with the baby. Do you think they think I'm doing a good job, too?"

- While putting together snacks for visitors, your client confides in you that they are feeling super guilty about not doing "the regular nap time routine" with their toddler and they feel like they are letting their "first baby" down.

- When chatting with your client about how they're feeling today, they say: "I'm so tired but I don't want to sleep because I'll be all alone in my room."

- On the way to your overnight, a client texts you the following: "Today has been exhausting. I'm ready to Netflix and chill in my bed. Baby was fed at 8:30. There are bottles in the fridge. I'm heading upstairs and will see you at 6:59am."

- Your client shares with you that they plan on a delayed vaccine schedule for their baby and they don't want to use the recommended schedule due to the high number of vaccines at each visit. They ask if you know a pediatrician that would be supportive of this approach.

- You arrive for your shift just as a group of people are leaving the client's home. Your client says to you: "It's so great to have my friends visiting; the house feels so full which I love but somehow I still feel so lonely."

- A client shares with you that they are feeling very conflicted because their sister-in-law said that pacifiers are a sleep crutch but they have also read research that states that pacifiers can reduce the risk of SIDS.

Remember that each client is an individual with their own unique personality. While you will likely notice a primary personality style, these DISC styles are fluid and are not one size fits all. Some people may present with several personality styles; other people might have a more dominant style depending on the situation they are in. The above scenarios are meant to help familiarize you with what it might be like to work with certain types but will obviously vary based on your situation.

NOTES:

Always Provide Non-Judgmental Support

A judgmental person is someone who categorizes people based on observations. Judgment comes in the form of actions and facial expressions, as well as verbal communication. By pure definition there can be a positive and a negative side to passing judgment. For example, parents may not categorize their parenting style because they are not familiar with the terms. By observing the way they care for their baby or keep to schedules, as a doula, you can "judge" that they lean more towards attachment parenting than scheduled parenting or vice versa.

By using non-judgmental support we can make observations that lead to decisions about how to best support the client. When working with a new family, it is important to remember that they may be feeling insecure about their expectations or ideas regarding parenting. They are being judged by family members and friends regarding every detail they share. From baby names to breast pumps, everyone has an opinion...except you, their doula.

The doula is there to support. They offer options and resources for clients to make the best choices for themselves and they encourage their clients to embrace those choices.

Validation is the key to empowering a new parent

Think of a time when you felt judged.

List 3 words that describe how being judged made you feel:

_____
_____
_____

Being judgment-free is not easy. It takes considerable effort on your part. During difficult times, remember that pregnancy, birth, and having a baby is a personal experience and the doula's role is to enhance the experience as much as possible for the client.

Listening Styles

Listening is what turns words, sentences, and paragraphs into communication.

Effective listening requires complete focus and attention. It includes noting the physical and emotional changes of the speaker's body language and the changes in the tone of their voice.

Active Listening

When we actively listen we are focused and attentive. We give verbal or non-verbal feedback by asking questions and/or by repeating back what the speaker has said.

"So, what I'm hearing you say is...."

Active listening is the most effective form of listening. The active listener is conveying to the person who is speaking that they acknowledge their thoughts, emotions, and feelings. Active listening is to be used when communicating with clients, as your understanding of their thoughts, feelings, and emotions is crucial to your ability to provide them with support.

Active Listening Tip: The 4 As

Becoming an exceptional active listener will take practice. To improve this skill, use the 4 As when conversing with clients:

Ask, Acknowledge, Ask, and Affirm

- Ask - As a client shares with you, ask pointed questions back to them to show that you are listening and absorbing everything they are telling you. For example, "Tell me more about what you are struggling with when it comes to breastfeeding?"
- Acknowledge - Next, acknowledge for the client that you have heard what they are expressing. "It sounds like the nipple pain is the worst thing right now. I know that must be difficult for you."
- Ask - Once again direct questions back to your client so they can convey to you how they are feeling. "Would you like to try a different breastfeeding position to see if that will help with the nipple pain?"
- Affirm - Finally, affirm that you have heard them and validate any

feelings and emotions they have shared with you. "I understand how painful this is right now. We will come up with a plan to help fix this. You are working so hard to feed your baby and should be so proud of yourself."

Passive Listening

In passive listening, while we are interested in hearing and understanding the other person's point of view, we are passively listening. This means we are assuming our understanding rather than confirming it.

The speaker may or may not feel "heard" and cannot be certain that a passive listener truly understands (or wants to understand) exactly what they are saying.

Combative Listening

Combative listeners are waiting to "attack." They are waiting for the speaker to pause so that they may assertively "share" their own opinions, rather than working to understand the speaker's point of view.

This type of listening is never appropriate during client interactions.

Understanding the Subtext of the Birth Story

Sometimes we share a story or recount an experience and without saying, "I felt like _____," an **active listener** can "hear" those feelings and take the next step to be certain they have heard correctly.

When we listen effectively, the "subtext" can become more clear. We can see facial expressions and body language that can contribute to our understanding. That is how a doula listens. A doula is looking to care for the client in a way that creates positive thoughts, feelings, and memories around the postpartum experience.

When someone tells their birth story and it includes something like:

> "My contractions were 2 minutes apart and really strong so we went to the hospital."
> "My partner brought me upstairs to the labor and delivery room and then he went to park the car."
> "They put me in a room and told me to put the gown on, when I came out of the bathroom, there was no one there."
> "I could hear a patient screaming in the room next door."

What kind of feelings do you think an experience like this might evoke?

Without suggesting how that client may have felt, it is imperative that you get an understanding of the feelings that were associated with those events.

Use the 4 As to gain a better understanding of this client's birth story.

Ask:

- "What were you thinking when you were on your way to the hospital?"
- "Were you comfortable with your partner leaving to park the car?"
- "When you came out of the bathroom and saw no one in the room, what did you do?"

Acknowledge:

- "It sounds like being at the hospital was going to make you feel safer."

- "Based on what you're saying, it sounds like you felt really strong and empowered!"

Ask:

- "How did you feel when you heard the other person screaming?"

Affirm:

- "It sounds like those screams pushed you to dig deep and find your own power. Good for you!"

Sometimes the way a client experiences things is not at all how the doula expects; using the 4 As will allow you to hear a client without imposing your own judgments.

Determining the "subtext" of your client's birth story and really understanding it can help you to more effectively provide support as their postpartum doula.

If you learn that the client is frightened or anxious when they do not understand something, they may feel best when they have knowledge and education on each new event in their postpartum life. If you learn that the client feels inadequate when people tell them what to do, supporting them as they form their own conclusions will contribute to their empowerment.

The "subtext" is an important part of any story. Use your active listening skills to be sure you have a complete understanding of each client's perspective on their own experience.

Postpartum Planning Session

A postpartum planning session is an opportunity to better prepare your clients for their transition into the postpartum period. It also enables you to gain a clear understanding of their goals so that you can determine the most effective way to support them.

It is best to conduct this planning session at the start of your first shift with a new client. By doing so, you will position yourself as an expert, rather than someone who simply performs a string of tasks around the home. This will help shape your client's expectations of your support and will set the tone for emotional, educational, and physical support.
While the below is certainly not an exhaustive list of questions or topics to explore, you can use these sample questions to help guide you while conducting a planning session.

Physical Support/Considerations:

- Are there any concerns surrounding you or your partner's physical health that could impact the early postpartum period?
- When will you be ready to welcome visitors into your home? Who will those people be?
- How will those early visitors help during the postpartum adjustment period?
- How would you describe those visitors' attitudes surrounding your feeding choices and parenting styles?
- What areas of your home are set up for comfort and healing? What changes need to be made to enable that?
- How is your home currently set up to support your feeding, sleeping, and care goals for your baby?
- How much parental leave do both parents have? What will daytime and nighttime support look like when your partner returns to work?

Emotional Support/Considerations:

- Are there any concerns surrounding you or your partner's mental health that could impact the early postpartum period? If so, are you already under the care of a mental health provider? Or do you need resources for providers?
- How does the early emotional adjustment to postpartum compare to how you imagined this would feel? How are you coping with

any variations?
- Emotionally, how are both parents adjusting to lack of sleep? How will prolonged lack of sleep affect your mental health?
- How well are both parents communicating with each other during this time? Are both parents on the same page with feeding/sleeping/newborn care goals and philosophies?

Educational Support/Considerations:

- How prepared do you feel when it comes to understanding your postpartum physical recovery? Are there any areas where you desire more education?
- Do you know how to spot red flags for your postpartum physical recovery?
- Did you take a newborn care class or infant feeding class prior to the baby's birth?
- How well do you feel like those classes prepared you for the early postpartum?
- Are there any topics surrounding newborn care for which you would like more education or support?
- How confident do you and your partner feel when it comes to caring for your newborn?
- Are there any worries or anxieties you have around this?
- When it comes to meeting both your short term feeding goals and your long term feeding goals, do you need any more education or support?
- Are there any topics surrounding newborn sleep for which you would like more education or support?

Emotional Adjustment to Parenthood

Many expectant parents take a childbirth class to prepare for birth. Some even take a newborn care class to familiarize themselves with what to expect from their new baby. But very few pregnant individuals understand, or know how to prepare for, the huge emotional adjustment they will face during the postpartum period.

Thus, you may encounter a client that is struggling with unrealistic expectations, overwhelmed with doubt, and reeling from judgmental comments expressed by friends and family. Other clients may feel frustrated by their inability to control this new environment they've found themselves in. All of this, coupled with exhaustion and physical discomfort, can greatly impact your client's emotional state.

Remember your foundational doula skills and your primary focus as a Postpartum & Infant Care Doula. Guiding and supporting your clients through this emotional adjustment is one of your main goals and why your support is so valuable.

Emotional support is the art of providing comfort to another person through reassurance, understanding, and encouragement. It is being sensitive to someone else's situation and recognizing their struggle. The person providing the support has no agenda other than to be supportive. They do not wish the person was not having a reaction and they do not try to fix the situation. They simply support the person where they are.

Avoid using phrases like:

> "I know how you feel."
> "Don't worry about it."
> "Look at the bright side."

Through attunement, non-judgmental support, and active listening, you will assist in building your client's confidence, helping them to eliminate self-judgment, and validating them on this common, yet overwhelming, emotional rollercoaster.

Social Media and Parenthood

Another area where your clients might be struggling with external and internal judgment is with social media "pressure." In today's world of social media, issues of judgment are more common as parents receive feedback from not just a select few members of their family or social group, but from hundreds or even thousands of people in online parenting groups.

It is impossible to find one group on social media where everyone agrees about what is best and there are no disagreements, especially when it comes to parenting.

As Postpartum & Infant Care Doulas, we may be called upon to help our clients deal with the emotional thoughts and feelings that these types of judgments can cause. Some clients may feel like they are not doing as good of a job as other parents that they interact with online.

Social media is a place where you can be led to believe someone is doing extremely well while they suffer in silence. Encourage clients not to judge how they feel on the inside against how people make themselves seem on the outside through social media.

We are present for our clients. We can validate their feelings and remind them that on these platforms, people only show the best parts of their lives, not the hard moments that are filled with doubt and frustration.

Encourage them to remember that when it comes to decisions they make as parents, it's easy to forget that one person doing it differently doesn't mean they are doing it better.

Supporting the Client:

D	Ask, "What have you decided you will do about this (any situation)?"
I	"I will be by your side through this whole thing, you can count on my support."
S	Ask, "Have you talked to your partner about this? Or other family members that you trust?"
C	"I am happy to do some research on this for you if you'd like?"

D	I	S	C
Dominant	Inspirational	Supportive	Cautious
Driven	Influential	Submissive	Competent
Demanding	Induces emotion	Stable	Calculating
Determined	Impressive	Security minded	Concerned
Decisive	Interactive	Sentimental	Compliant
Delegates	Interested in people	Safe	Contemplative

Notes:

Perinatal Mood & Anxiety Disorders

Postpartum mood and anxiety disorders (PMADs) are not a character flaw or a weakness! Sometimes it is simply a complication of giving birth. Many newly delivered clients experience the "baby blues" after childbirth, which commonly include mood swings and crying spells that fade quickly. But some new parents experience more severe, long-lasting forms of mood and anxiety disorders. In many cases, clients do not want to admit to having these feelings, so they may try to hide them.

As a doula, it is important for you to be aware of the signs and symptoms of the various PMADs, as well as their levels of severity. A doula must also have proper resources available to assist a new family in finding the support that they need.

As doulas, we are not universally mandated reporters so we must each as individuals rely on our intuition when a situation that includes postpartum emotional issues occurs. The staff at ProDoula is always available if you find yourself needing to discuss or process a situation regarding the best way to support a client.

Postpartum Psychosis

Postpartum psychosis is a rare condition that can develop within 2-4 weeks after giving birth with a typical onset between 3-10 days post delivery. It is most common in those who have given birth for the first time. The biggest risk factor includes a personal history of bipolar disorder. Most individuals who experience postpartum psychosis will later develop or be diagnosed with this disorder. The signs and symptoms are very severe and this client requires immediate medical attention as they are at an increased risk of suicide and infanticide.

• Worry • Confusion and disorientation • Mania	• Hallucinations (auditory/visual) • Delusions	• Paranoia • Thoughts/attempts to harm self or baby

Postpartum Post-Traumatic Stress Disorder (PTSD)

Postpartum PTSD can occur from a traumatic experience before or during childbirth or in the postpartum period. It is important to note that the trauma can be real or perceived; all that matters is that the client experienced the event as traumatic.

• Re-experiencing the experience • Flashbacks	• Nightmares • Anxiety • Irritability or hypervigilance	• Avoidance of any person, thing, or event that could be triggering

Postpartum Obsessive Compulsive Disorder (OCD)

Postpartum OCD is most often characterized by the presence of intrusive thoughts - vivid images that involve harm coming to the client or their baby. These intrusive thoughts can manifest as compulsions over the baby's health and wellness and can involve repeating certain tasks multiple times (bathing, diapering, etc.). This could lead to harm to the client and/or the child. It is important to note, though, that clients experiencing postpartum OCD have not lost touch with reality, unlike clients experiencing postpartum psychosis, and they know these vivid images are not real.

• Intrusive thoughts • Obsessions around these thoughts	• Compulsive behaviors • Fear of being alone with baby	• Over-protective of baby

Postpartum Rage

Postpartum rage is defined as aggression, agitation, and intense anger during the weeks or months after birth. It is most common within the first six weeks after birth but can be experienced during the first year postpartum. Exact statistics on the frequency of postpartum rage are not available as this topic is not well researched and the symptoms are often seen as an extension of postpartum depression.

As research is limited, an exact cause of postpartum rage has not been determined. However, causes are likely associated with lack of sleep or changes in sleep patterns, body, lifestyle, and relationship changes and a decrease in estrogen and progesterone levels post-birth.

• Losing control of one's temper	• Screaming or yelling more than usual • Lashing out or "flipping out"	• Feeling unable to cope with one's emotions

Postpartum Anxiety

Like postpartum depression, the symptoms of postpartum anxiety are often more intense and longer lasting than just the "baby blues." Many clients struggling with postpartum anxiety are plagued by constant worry and may experience acute panic attacks. This client should be encouraged to reach out to their health care provider to discuss treatment options.

• Worry • Racing thoughts • Irritability or rage	• Inability to sleep • Loss of appetite	• Physical symptoms such as dizziness or nausea

Postpartum Depression

Signs and symptoms are more intense and longer lasting than just the "baby blues." They can severely interfere with the client's ability to care for their baby or handle daily tasks. This client likely needs to be seen by their care provider.

• Loss of appetite • Insomnia • Intense irritability and anger	• Overwhelming fatigue • Feelings of shame, guilt, or inadequacy • Severe mood swings	• Difficulty bonding with baby • Withdrawal from friends and family • Thoughts of harming self or baby

Baby Blues Symptoms

While the baby blues are considered the least severe form of depression, the impact is still powerful for newly postpartum individuals. For those who experience the baby blues it is common for them to experience confusion surrounding the sadness and depression they may have been feeling when the expectation of society is that one should be happy and joyous about the arrival of their new baby. The exact cause (as with most

PMADs) remains unknown, but is often attributed to fluctuations in hormones, lack or disruption of sleep, the disruption of previous life routines, and emotions surrounding the birthing experience as a whole.

Baby blues typically last from a few days to two or three weeks. This client can benefit tremendously from postpartum doula support. Help them with good and delicious nutrition, proper hydration, and the opportunity to get a little bit of extra sleep.

• Mood swings • Anxiety • Sadness	• Irritability • Crying • Trouble sleeping	• Decreased concentration • Fatigue

Prevalence of Perinatal Mood Disorders	
Antepartum Depression and Antepartum Anxiety	15-21%
Postpartum Depression	21%
Postpartum Panic Disorder	Up to 11%
Postpartum Obsessive Compulsive Disorder	Up to 11%
Postpartum Post-Traumatic Stress Disorder	9%
Postpartum Psychosis	1-2 of every 1,000

Source: Postpartum Support International

Perinatal mental health conditions, such as depression, anxiety, and OCD, can have an impact on the bond between the baby and the parent and the infant's health.

During pregnancy, depression can restrict the growth of the fetus, resulting in smaller babies and slower fetal growth. Clients who suffer from antenatal depression are also more likely to give birth prematurely and to a low birth weight baby. The children of clients who experienced depression during pregnancy have a higher incidence of developmental delays, suffer sleep disturbances, and are more likely to be overweight. (Field, T. (2010)

After birth, the infants of depressed clients are less responsive to stimulus, and when not properly diagnosed and treated, postpartum depression can cause a disruption in bonding between the client and the baby. Clients who are depressed are more likely to smoke, miss well-child visits, use the emergency room as a source of health care for the infant, and use corporal punishment.

Additionally, when a client becomes overwhelmed by postpartum mood and anxiety disorders they are less likely to breastfeed and are less likely to follow the advice of the infant's doctors for managing any chronic health problems or disabilities the baby may have. The client is also less likely to spend time engaged with the infant through touch. (Meohler, E. 2006)

The Edinburgh Postnatal Depression Scale is a self assessment tool that can be used with postpartum individuals to assess their risk for PMADs. We have included a copy of this assessment on the following pages.

As a Postpartum & Infant Care Doula, it is not within your scope to diagnose postpartum mood disorders. It is within your scope to provide clients with resources and referrals back to their providers for more information and diagnosis. The tool provided on the next page can be given to all postpartum clients as part of the information and resources you may provide.

The Experience of PMADs Among Non-Birthing Parents

According to an article published in the Journal of Neuropsychiatric Disease and Treatment in February of 2023, up to 8-10% of non-birthing parents will experience PMADs. Unfortunately, the diagnosis of PMADs in the non-birthing individual is often delayed or complicated by the lack of consistent healthcare as opposed to that of the birthing parent. Other factors that complicate diagnosis and treatment include gender differences in how PMADs manifest and the social stigmas that still exist surrounding seeking help and receiving treatment for mental health related disorders.

Perinatal Mental Health Disorders: A Review of Lessons Learned from Obstetric Care Settings
Nina K Ayala, et. al, February 2023

When PMADs are experienced by partners they can arise from:

- Feelings of powerlessness
- Perception of loss of control
    - These feelings often come from differences between expectation and realities in relation to parenting
    - Trying to balance their individual needs with that of the birthing parent and their child(ren)

- Trying to balance the needs of work vs family
- Changes in their relationship with the birthing person
- Conflicting messages about their parental role and involvement from society

Source: Developing an intervention for paternal perinatal depression: An international Delphi study, Journal of Affective Disorders Reports, Volume 2, 2020

The identification and treatment of PMADs in the non-birthing parent is still in its infancy and has historically focused on male identifying, heterosexual partners. More research is needed to include same sex partners although current available information demonstrates that many of the root causes for PMADs are similar among both demographics.

FDA Approves First Oral Treatment for Postpartum Depression

In August of 2023 the US Food and Drug Administration approved the medication Zurzuvae, the first oral pill for the treatment of postpartum depression.

Before the approval of this oral medication the only other treatment targeted to postpartum depression was the drug Zulresso, which was an IV infusion that required hospital admission and was administered over the span of 60 hours. With a cost of $35,000, lack of universal insurance coverage, and side effects made IV treatment with Zulresso difficult for many to obtain.

Zurzuvae is a 14 day oral course of medication that is to be taken once a day, in the evening with a "fatty meal," according to the FDA. Clinical trials of Zurzuvae have demonstrated rapid improvement in the symptoms of depression by day 15 and as early as day 3. The effects of the 14 day course of medication have been shown in clinical trials to continue to be effective through the 45 day follow up period that was a part of the clinical trials.

While this medication holds much promise, cost and insurance coverage may still be a barrier to this form of treatment for many postpartum individuals. The 14 day course of treatment has an associated cost of $16,000. As a result, Medicaid and other insurance carriers may require an attempt of treatment with a more cost effective medication before authorizing and covering the cost of Zurzuvae.

Sage Therapeutics, who manufactures Zurzuvae, have indicated that they will work with insurance companies to make the medication more ac-

Edinburgh Postnatal Depression Scale (EPDS)

Name: _____ Your Date of Birth: _____
Baby's Date of Birth: _____ Date Assessment Given: _____
Address: _____
Phone: _____ OB/Midwife Phone: _____

As you are pregnant or have recently had a baby, we would like to know how you are feeling. Please check the answer that comes closest to how you have felt IN THE PAST 7 DAYS, not just how you feel today. Here is an example, already completed.

I have felt happy:

☐ Yes, all the time	(0)	☑ Yes, most of the time	(1)
☐ No, not very often	(2)	☐ No, not at all	(3)

In the past 7 days:
This would mean: "I have felt happy most of the time" during the past week.

Please complete the following 10 questions in the same way.
1. I have been able to laugh and see the funny side of things

☐ As much as I always could	(0)	☐ Not quite so much now	(1)
☐ Definitely not so much now	(2)	☐ Not at all	(3)

2. I have looked forward with enjoyment to things

☐ As much as I ever did	(0)	☐ Rather less than I used to	(1)
☐ Definitely less than I used to	(2)	☐ Hardly at all	(3)

*3. I have blamed myself unnecessarily when things went wrong

☐ Yes, most of the time	(0)	☐ Yes, some of the time	(1)
☐ Not very often	(2)	☐ No, never	(3)

4. I have been anxious or worried for no good reason

☐ No, not at all	(0)	☐ Hardly ever	(1)
☐ Yes, sometimes	(2)	☐ Yes, very often	(3)

*5. I have felt scared or panicky for no very good reason

| ☐ Yes, quite a lot | (0) | ☐ Yes, sometimes | (1) |
| ☐ No, not much | (2) | ☐ No, not at all | (3) |

*6. Things have been getting on top of me

| ☐ Yes, most of the time I haven't been able to cope at all | (0) | ☐ Yes, sometimes I haven't been coping as well as usual | (1) |
| ☐ No, most of the time I have coped quite well | (2) | ☐ No, I have been coping as well as ever | (3) |

*7. I have been so unhappy that I have had difficulty sleeping

| ☐ Yes, most of the time I haven't been able to cope at all | (0) | ☐ Yes, sometimes I haven't been coping as well as usual | (1) |
| ☐ No, most of the time I have coped quite well | (2) | ☐ No, I have been coping as well as ever | (3) |

*8. I have felt sad or miserable

| ☐ Yes, most of the time | (0) | ☐ Yes, quite often | (1) |
| ☐ Not very often | (2) | ☐ No, not at all | (3) |

*9. I have been so unhappy that I have been crying

| ☐ Yes, most of the time | (0) | ☐ Yes, quite often | (1) |
| ☐ Only occasionally | (2) | ☐ No, never | (3) |

*10. The thought of harming myself has occurred to me

| ☐ Yes, quite often | (0) | ☐ Sometimes | (1) |
| ☐ Hardly ever | (2) | ☐ Never | (3) |

Total Score: _____ Date of Assessment: _____

Scoring

QUESTIONS 1, 2, & 4 (without an *) Are scored 0, 1, 2 or 3 with top left box scored as 0 and the bottom right box scored as 3.

QUESTIONS 3, 5-10 (marked with an *) Are reverse scored, with the top left box scored as a 3 and the bottom right box scored as 0.

Maximum score: 30

Possible Depression: 10 or greater

Always look at item 10 (suicidal thoughts)

Instructions for using the Edinburgh Postnatal Depression Scale:

1. The client is asked to check the response that comes closest to how they have been feeling in the previous 7 days.
2. All the items must be completed.
3. Care should be taken to avoid the possibility of the client discussing the answers with others. (Answers come from the pregnant/postpartum person.)
4. The client should complete the scale themselves, unless they have limited English or have difficulty with reading.

Users may reproduce the scale without further permission providing they respect copyright by quoting the names of the authors, the title, and the source of the paper in all reproduced copies. Edinburgh Postnatal Depression Scale 1 (EPDS)

Source: Cox, J.L., Holden, J.M., and Sagovsky, R. 1987. Detection of postnatal depression: Development of the 10-item Edinburgh Postnatal Depression Scale. British Journal of Psychiatry 150:782-786.

Source: K. L. Wisner, B. L. Parry, C. M. Piontek, Postpartum Depression N Engl J Med vol. 347, No 3, July 18, 2002, 194-199.

Supportive Dos and Don'ts Do:

Do

- Encourage physical activity such as a walk with the baby.
- Encourage healthy foods and to avoid drinking alcohol.
- Encourage the client to take time for themselves or with their partner.
- Focus the client on positive situations and realistic expectations.

Don't:

- Try to diagnose the client.
- Suggest treatments or drugs.
- Compare the client to other clients.

There is no single cause of PMADs. Physical, emotional, hormonal, and lifestyle factors may all play a role.

Ask yourself these questions:

- "Does the client appear to be happy at the appropriate times?"
- "Is the client getting more and more comfortable with their baby?"
- "Is the client resting when they are tired? Are they able to rest?"
- "Does the client appear to be bonding with their baby?"

Build a network of resources to refer clients to when necessary.

Supporting the client:

D	Be direct. Ask how they are feeling both physically and emotionally.
I	Remind the client that you are there for them and they can share anything with you. Ask how they have been feeling emotionally.
S	Praise their commitment to their family and ask if there is anything upsetting them.
C	Suggest they keep a journal regarding their recovery and their feelings. Let them know you have the best resources available for anything they may need.

The Early Postpartum Period

For the newly postpartum client, the early days with a newborn can fluctuate between feeling on top of the world and feeling a complete loss of control. While the person is no longer pregnant, they may still look and feel like they are. While labor has certainly ended, and the baby is obviously here, the uterus is still contracting. Additionally, the attention from others has shifted from the pregnant person to the new baby and the client may not be ready for that.

As doulas, we recognize that the early postpartum period is actually an extension of pregnancy, labor, and birth. We acknowledge that our clients are still experiencing the physical changes of pregnancy while adapting to the emotional changes of the postpartum period.

Physical changes that occur during pregnancy and birth:

- Weight gain - anywhere from 25-80 lbs
- Bodily exhaustion and changes - linea nigra, varicose veins, etc.
- Physical pain
- Increased urination
- Difficulty sleeping
- Swelling
- Changes in bowel movements

Those who have recently given birth may feel some of the following emotional changes:

- Weepy
- Excited
- Doubtful
- Anxious
- Fearful
- As if they are on a hormonal roller coaster

Once the client has a chance to catch their stride in the transition between pregnancy and parenting they will then be able to mentally and physically separate these aspects of their life.

Notes:

Physical Recovery from Birth

In the United States, it is not uncommon for expectant families to focus more on securing necessary items for their baby's arrival and on planning for the birth than on how they will manage the challenges of the early postpartum period.

However, in many other countries planning for the recovery period post birth is quite customary.

Countries such as Belgium and the Netherlands incorporate postpartum planning into their pregnancy care starting at around 34 weeks gestation. Finland is the most well known country for their attention to the importance of maternity and postpartum care. Once a pregnant individual has reached 22 weeks of pregnancy they can apply for the famous "baby box" from the social security system. This box, which doubles as an infant bed, includes over 63 essentials for the baby.

In these non-US countries, planning for the postpartum period begins during pregnancy.

When viewed across cultures, the postpartum period is typically defined as the first 40 days. However, depending on the culture, the postpartum individual may be viewed as "unclean" or "vulnerable." Patriarchal cultures historically viewed the postpartum person as unclean or a threat to their surroundings and separated them from others, while other cultures viewed the surroundings as a potential threat to the person.

Regardless of the underpinning culture, separating the birthing person also brought with it a time to rest, recover, and be cared for by others.

In Muslim culture, newly postpartum individuals are mandated to 40 days of rest. During this time others will tend to the daily tasks of caring for the home and family. They will have a special postpartum diet prepared for them, as well as guidelines that indicate that they must avoid the wind, stay indoors, and not take baths.

Latin America follows the mandated 40 days of rest also. In this culture, other individuals will attend to the daily tasks of running the home and feeding the family. Some family cultures will include special meals for the newly postpartum individual.

In China, 30 days of rest is indicated. The birthing person will have assistance with caring for the task of the home and help with the newborn. They will be fed meals that warm the body, consisting of hot drinks and foods. Japanese culture brings the birthing person back to their parents' home to be cared for by their family. After a few months in their parents' home they return to their husband's family with a new social status that is often marked by the giving of gifts to the newly postpartum individual. Nigerian culture is particularly interesting. Here the newly postpartum individual is sent to what is called a "fattening room." In this space the newly postpartum individual's only role is to recover by gaining weight, sleeping, and looking after their baby for two to three months. The Masai tribe in Kenya and Tanzania also have similar customs in which the birthing person's only role is to remain isolated and "eat in abundance."

We also see Viking communities historically impose a period of confinement on postpartum individuals to protect them from evil spirits that were believed to lurk in the waterways, woods, and hills. They were cared for by others who tended to their homes and fed a postpartum porridge called "barselgrøt." Because they were considered both unclean and vulnerable to evil spirits the newly postpartum individual was secluded for 40 days, however, not left alone, especially at night, which meant that other (female) family members and friends took turns sitting with the postpartum individual and helping with caring for their baby.

Source: Postnatal care: A cross-cultural and historical perspective, 2010)

In the United States, rituals and customs surrounding the postnatal period largely fell by the wayside when birth was moved from the home to the hospital, around the 1950s. Postpartum customs were replaced by the 6 week postnatal visit, which is approximately 40 days post-birth.

In the 1950s post birth hospital stays of up to 14 days were not uncommon. By the 1960s this window had shortened to no less than 8 days. During this time the birthing person and the baby were cared for and monitored with the baby being brought to the birthing parent every 4 hours to feed. Otherwise, the parent's role was to rest and recover. Currently in the United States, the average hospital stay post vaginal or cesarean delivery is 2.7 days.

Source: Postnatal care: A cross-cultural and historical perspective, 2010

Unlike other countries that have systems in place for home visits from medical professionals such as nurses, midwives, and social workers, newly delivered individuals who give birth vaginally will not see their care provider again until the 6 week follow up visit.

This underscores the importance of the Postpartum & Infant Care Doula having a firm foundation of knowledge surrounding what is normal and what is beyond the scope of normal when working with newly postpartum individuals. The doula may be the first to potentially identify an issue that is beyond the scope of normal that should be addressed by a medical or mental health provider.

Physical and Emotional Recovery from Birth - The First Six Weeks	
Physical	**Emotional**
Week 1:	
<ul><li>The uterus will contract and return to its pre-pregnancy state.</li><li>Vaginal bleeding - menstrual-like with some clotting.<ul><li>Vaginal Delivery<ul><li>Vaginal/perineal soreness and/or swelling</li></ul></li><li>Cesarean Delivery<ul><li>Pain/discomfort at incision site</li><li>Lower abdominal discomfort when moving</li><li>Movement encouraged to prevent blood clots</li></ul></li></ul></li><li>Lactogenesis II is initiated upon delivery of the placenta.<ul><li>Milk volume in the breasts will rapidly increase from 38 to 98 hours post birth.<ul><li>The breasts may begin to feel warm and full.</li></ul></li></ul></li><li>Nipple discomfort during breastfeeding is not uncommon.<ul><li>If there is pain, cracked or bleeding nipples, or other issues encourage a consultation with a lactation consultant.</li></ul></li></ul>	<ul><li>Fluctuations in hormones can cause feelings of overwhelm.</li><li>Exhaustion begins to set in.</li><li>The third day post birth can be particularly difficult with a culmination of exhaustion and hormonal shifts.</li></ul>

Physical and Emotional Recovery from Birth - The First Six Weeks	
Physical	**Emotional**
Week 2:	

- Itching in the areas surrounding perineal trauma, such as tearing or episiotomy, and itching around the cesarean incision.
- Decrease in the amount of vaginal bleeding.
- Continued soreness/tenderness around the cesarean incision is expected.
- Movement post-cesarean becomes easier.
- Lactogenesis III begins around day nine.
  - In order for the breasts to continue to make milk, milk must be removed.
    - Milk may be removed via direct feeding at the breasts or pumping.
- Nipple tenderness or discomfort during breastfeeding may be present.
	- Some individuals will experience the baby blues.
	  - Red flags that require the attention of a medical professional include: complete overwhelm, difficulty bonding with the baby, suicidal thoughts, or thoughts of harming the baby.
	- Feelings surrounding the birth experience may begin to emerge, especially if the outcome was unanticipated or the experience was perceived as traumatic.

Physical and Emotional Recovery from Birth - The First Six Weeks	
Physical	**Emotional**
Week 3-5:	
• Continued soreness/tenderness around the cesarean incision is expected but should gradually improve week over week. • Postpartum bleeding will continue to taper off and change from bright red to pinkish-brown to clear. • An increase in bleeding can be an indicator that the postpartum person is doing too much. • Many breastfeeding individuals may find that feeding issues at the breast have begun to resolve.	• Some individuals may experience symptoms of postpartum depression • Feelings surrounding the birth experience may begin to emerge, especially if the first few weeks were filled with challenges that required focus and attention of the birthing person, i.e., sick baby, challenges with postpartum recovery, breastfeeding, etc.

Physical and Emotional Recovery from Birth - The First Six Weeks	
Physical	**Emotional**
Week 6:	
<ul><li>The uterus has returned to pre-pregnancy size.</li><li>Vaginal bleeding related to birth has stopped.</li><li>Menses may return.</li><li>Most individuals are cleared for</li><li>return to sexual activity and moderate exercise at the 6 week follow up visit.</li><li>Post cesarean recovery, most individuals are cleared to return to normal daily activities and lifting.<ul><li>The incision site may continue to be itchy and/or numb.</li></ul></li><li>Those who have chosen to breastfeed or pump will need to continue to remove milk to signal the body to make more milk.<ul><li>This stage of lactation is called galactopoiesis and refers to the maintenance of an established milk supply.</li></ul></li></ul>	<ul><li>Ongoing feelings of exhaustion are normal.</li><li>Some individuals feel that they are finding their sense of rhythm with baby care and parenting.</li></ul>

Postpartum Discharge Instructions

For many new parents, the time spent in the hospital or birth facility is a whirlwind. With little to no sleep, they labor and give birth, meet their new baby for the first time, and begin to tackle infant feeding. On the day of their discharge, they are given oral and written discharge instructions that can seem a bit overwhelming. Some parents report not remembering that they received this information at all.

As a Postpartum & Infant Care Doula, you must be familiar with routine postpartum discharge instructions that most birthing individuals will receive at discharge. This will enable you to answer questions that may arise and be on the lookout for any potential red flags.

What to Expect After Birth

- Bleeding from the vagina is expected after vaginal or cesarean birth
- Passing of small blood clots upon standing is considered normal
- Bleeding will become less red, will transition to pink, and then brown, yellow, and clear
- Weight loss of up to 20 pounds over the first two weeks
- The uterus should be hard and round and felt just below the belly button
- Breast engorgement is common
- If the person is not breastfeeding, engorgement should resolve within a few days
- Wearing a supportive bra for the first 1-2 weeks is helpful
- Avoiding nipple stimulation will be beneficial
- Ice/cold packs can help with discomfort
- Taking recommended medications to help decrease inflammation and pain is encouraged
- If client has had perineal trauma or an episiotomy:
  - They can return to normal household activities as they feel ready, for example light office work, housekeeping, or walking
  - Waiting until the six week follow up appointment to resume the use of tampons, engage in vaginal sexual activity, or resume moderate to high impact activities such as jogging, lifting weights, or dancing is recommended
- If client has had a cesarean birth:
  - Incision site should be kept clean and dry
  - Redness, oozing, or discharge warrants a call to their provider

- Using a pillow or belly band for support of the incision site can be helpful
- Unless otherwise indicated, sutures will dissolve, they do not need to be removed
- If client experiences constipation:
  - Eating a diet high in fiber with ample fruits and vegetables can be helpful
  - Consuming 8 cups of water a day to help prevent constipation and urinary
  - tract infections is recommended
  - If needed, a stool softener may be recommended
  - If any of the following are experienced, encourage the client to contact their provider:
  - Bleeding that soaks more than one pad an hour and/or blood clots passing that are larger than a golf ball
  - Experiencing heavy, menstrual-like bleeding after the 4th day of birth
  - Swelling or redness in either of the legs
  - Persistent fever of over 100 degrees F
  - Increased pain or tenderness in the belly or at the cesarean incision site
  - Increased pain in the perineum if client has had perineal trauma or an episiotomy
  - Vaginal discharge that becomes heavier and has a foul odor
  - Inability to care for themselves or their baby
  - Feelings of sadness, depression, wanting to withdraw, or thoughts or feelings of harming themself or their baby
  - Tender, red, or warm area on either breast
  - Signs of postpartum preeclampsia:
  - Swelling in the face, hands, or eyes
  - Sudden weight gain of more than 2 pounds in one week
  - A headache that will not go away or becomes progressively worse
  - Vision changes such as:
  - Flashing lights
  - Loss of vision
  - Light sensitivity
  - Blurry vision
  - Body pain or aches associated with a fever

Vaginal Soreness

In 2009, the National Hospital Discharge Survey reported that approximately 24.5% of birthing individuals had received an episiotomy during the delivery of their baby. In 2006, the American College of Obstetricians and Gynecologists revised their practice guidelines to recommend against routine episiotomy. According to the Leapfrog Hospital Survey, data shows that in 2022, 4.8% of vaginal births involved episiotomy, a marked decrease from the 12.5% reported in 2012.

In some communities this number may be vastly higher or lower. The American College of Obstetricians and Gynecologists reports that between 53-79% of vaginal births will result in some degree of vaginal tearing. If your client has had an episiotomy or tear, it is important to know that the wound may be painful or tender for a period of time. Extensive tears will take longer to heal and will require more support.

In the meantime, you can coach the client to help promote healing:

- Soothe the wound. Encourage the client to soothe the wound by placing a chilled sanitary pad against their perineum.
- Take the sting out of urination. Suggest the client pour warm water over the vulva during urination.
- Take the pressure off of pushing. Have the client press a clean pad firmly against the wound when bearing down for a bowel movement.
- Keep the wound clean. Remind the client to use a peri bottle filled with warm water to rinse the tissue between the vaginal opening and anus (perineum) after using the toilet.
- Sit down carefully. If the client finds sitting uncomfortable, encourage them to sit on a soft surface and place a small pillow or rolled up towel under one side of the buttocks to elevate their bottom.

While the client is healing, they can expect the discomfort to progressively improve. It is advised to have them contact their health care provider if the pain intensifies, the wound becomes hot, swollen, and painful, or they notice any pus-like discharge.

Vaginal Discharge

Clients will have a vaginal discharge (lochia) for a number of weeks after delivery. Expect a bright red, heavy flow of blood for the first few days. If they have been sitting or lying down, they might notice a small gush when they stand up. The discharge will gradually taper off, changing from pink or brown to yellow or white. To reduce the risk of infection, it is recommended that the client use sanitary napkins rather than tampons during this time.

Don't be alarmed if the client occasionally passes small blood clots. Have them contact their health care provider if:

- They soak a sanitary pad within an hour while lying down
- The discharge has a foul odor
- They pass clots larger than a golf ball
- They have a fever of 100.4° F (38° C) or higher

Contractions

Clients will likely feel uterine contractions, sometimes called "after pains," during the first few days following delivery. These contractions, which often resemble menstrual cramps, help to prevent excessive bleeding by compressing the blood vessels in the uterus. For reasons that are not entirely clear, these after pains tend to be stronger with successive deliveries. The client's health care provider may recommend an over-the-counter pain reliever if necessary.

Encourage the client to stay on top of the pain and not wait until the pain is too great to medicate. Have the client contact their healthcare provider if they have a fever or if their abdomen is tender to the touch. These signs and symptoms could indicate a uterine infection.

Postpartum Diaphoresis/Sweating

According to the Cleveland Clinic, up to 35% of newly postpartum individuals will experience excessive sweating, particularly at night. The trigger for these episodes is the shift in hormones during the early postpartum period and the fluids given during labor and birth. Estrogen levels decrease after birth, which signals the hypothalamus to believe that the body is too hot. As a result, it triggers the body to perspire in order to lower the core temperature. Breastfeeding can also serve as an additional trigger for night sweats as prolactin, the hormone responsible for the production of breastmilk, keeps estrogen levels low.

Those that experience postpartum sweating often find that the episodes resolve a few weeks after birth. It is important for the newly postpartum parent to drink plenty of fluids to help avoid dehydration. The use of cotton clothing and sheets can help create a cooler environment for the body.

Urination Problems

Swelling or bruising of the tissue surrounding the bladder and urethra can lead to difficulty when urinating. A client who is fearful of the sting of urine on the tender perineal area can have the same effect. Difficulty urinating usually resolves on its own. In the meantime, it will help to have the client pour warm water over their vulva with a peri bottle while they are sitting on the toilet.

Have the client contact their healthcare provider if they have any symptoms of a urinary tract infection. For example:

- It hurts to urinate
- The client doesn't feel like they are emptying their bladder fully
- They have an unusually frequent urge to urinate

Pregnancy and birth stretch the connective tissue at the base of the bladder and can cause nerve and muscle damage to the bladder or urethra. The client might leak urine when they cough, strain, or laugh.

Fortunately, this problem usually improves within three months. In the meantime, encourage them to wear sanitary pads to prevent any mess. If the problem does not improve, your client may wish to contact a pelvic floor therapist.

Hemorrhoids and Bowel Movements

If a client notices pain during bowel movements and experiences swelling near the anus, they might have hemorrhoids. These are stretched and swollen veins in the anus or lower rectum. To ease any discomfort during healing, the client can soak in a warm tub and apply chilled witch hazel pads to the affected area. Their healthcare provider may recommend a topical hemorrhoid medication as well.

If the client finds they are avoiding bowel movements out of fear of hurting their perineum or aggravating the pain of hemorrhoids or the episiotomy wound, encourage them to take steps to keep the stool soft and regular. Eating foods high in fiber, such as fruits, vegetables, and whole grains along with drinking plenty of water is an excellent start. They can ask their healthcare provider about a stool softener or fiber laxative if needed.

Another potential problem for those who have experienced an unusually long pushing phase is the inability to control bowel movements, also known as fecal incontinence. If the client has trouble controlling bowel movements they should consult their health care provider.

Cesarean Birth Recovery

The client who has had a cesarean birth should rest as much as possible for the first two weeks at home. Housework and social activity should be limited while recovering from surgery. The client should not climb stairs more than 2-3 times a day during the early recovery period. They should not lift anything heavier than the baby.

The client may return to their normal diet at home and should maintain excellent hydration. If elimination is difficult, encourage them to ask their provider about a mild laxative. The client can shower and wash their hair as normal unless otherwise instructed by the provider. They should not insert anything into the vagina (tampons, douche, etc.) until the provider affirms it is okay.

Have the client contact their healthcare provider if:

- There is swelling, redness, or increased pain in the incision area
- There is pus coming from the incision
- A bad smell is noticed from the incision or surgical dressing
- The incision is breaking open
- The client feels dizzy
- There is pain or bleeding during urination
- They experience diarrhea
- They experience nausea or vomiting
- There is abnormal vaginal discharge
- There is an abnormal or allergic reaction to any medicine
- If stronger pain medication becomes necessary

Hair Loss and Skin Changes

During pregnancy, elevated hormone levels put normal hair loss on hold. The result is often an extra-lush head of hair — but now it's payback time. After delivery, the body sheds the excess hair all at once. Within six months, the client's hair will most likely be back to normal. Stretch marks won't disappear after delivery, but eventually they'll fade from reddish purple to silver or white. The darkened line down the abdomen called "la linea nigra" will slowly fade as well.

Weight Loss

After the client gives birth, they will probably feel flabby and out of shape. They might even look like they are still pregnant. This is perfectly normal. Most postpartum individuals lose more than 10 pounds during birth, which includes the weight of the baby, placenta, and amniotic fluid. In the days after delivery, they will lose additional weight from leftover fluids. After that, a healthy diet and regular exercise can help them to gradually return to their pre-pregnancy weight.

The Postpartum Checkup

About six weeks after delivery the client's healthcare provider will check the vagina, cervix, and uterus to make sure they are healing well. The provider might do a breast exam and check the client's weight and blood pressure too. Prepare the client to talk about birth control options, as well as breastfeeding and how they are adjusting to life with a new baby. This appointment is short and clients don't always have much time to talk about what's really going on.

Postpartum Red Flags

As a Postpartum & Infant Care Doula, you should be aware of these postpartum red flags, which always require the help of the client's medical provider. Serious complications, such as heart failure, blood clots or aneurysms, postpartum hemorrhage, or postpartum preeclampsia, can arise after the client has been discharged from the hospital. These conditions must be taken seriously.

The client should seek IMMEDIATE medical care if:

- They develop signs of possible infection

- Fever of 100.0° F or higher
- Abdominal pain
- They develop signs of a possible deep vein thrombosis or pulmonary embolism
  - Chest pain
  - Shortness of breath
  - Fainting
  - Pain, swelling, or redness of the legs
- They develop signs of possible retained placental fragments
  - Heavy vaginal bleeding, with or without blood clots
  - Vaginal bleeding has a foul odor
- They develop signs of postpartum preeclampsia
  - Swelling of the face or hands
  - Sudden weight gain of 2+ pounds in a week
  - Visual disturbances such as seeing spots, blurry vision, temporary loss of vision
  - Persistent headache that does not get better or gets worse
- They develop signs of mastitis
  - Redness in the breast
  - Breast feels hot to the touch
  - Fever

Postpartum Red Flags - Quiz

The left column - numbered 1-7 - lists common side effects or symptoms that may occur during the postpartum recovery period, particularly in the early postpartum hours/days/weeks. The right column - lettered a-g - lists various postpartum issues.

Draw a line from the number on the left-hand side to the letter on the right-hand side that corresponds to the appropriate issue.

1) The client notices a build up of fluid and asymmetrical swelling in their legs.	a) Postpartum hemorrhage
	b) Retained placenta
2) The client is breastfeeding and begins running a fever and feels a hot, red spot on their breast.	c) Pulmonary embolism
	d) Mastitis
3) The client is experiencing blurry vision and is seeing spots.	e) Urinary tract infection
4) The client is passing golf ball size blood clots and has soaked through a new pad within one hour.	f) Postpartum preeclampsia
	g) Infected incision
5) The client is running a fever and has noticed a foul odor coming from the vaginal discharge.	
6) The client had a cesarean birth and has noticed a foul odor along with a pus-like discharge around the incision site.	
7) The client has an unusual urge to urinate frequently, does not feel like they can fully empty their bladder, and experiences pain when urinating.	

Infant Care

As a Postpartum & Infant Care Doula it is expected that you will be a trusted and educated resource for your clients when it comes to caring for their new baby. Your clients will have questions about infant care and feeding, what to expect when it comes to newborn behavioral and developmental milestones, how to soothe and comfort their new baby, and so much more. This is an area where clients may feel overwhelmed by unsolicited advice and the judgment of others. Your job is to provide unbiased support and evidence-based information so that new families can find the solutions that are right for them and grow more confident.

From time to time, a client may ask their doula which decisions they made specific to a certain topic, especially if they are struggling to make choices of their own. This can be a delicate conversation to navigate. It is acceptable to share your own experiences with your clients, if you are comfortable doing so, however, you may be hesitant to share if your own decisions vary widely from what you believe your client will choose. A doula never makes decisions for their clients or tells them how they should navigate a situation with their children, but rather, provides non-judgmental support to enable the parent to decide for themselves.

The support **BRA** can be a helpful tool for decision making in these instances. BRA stands for:

- Benefits
- Risks
- Alternatives

Helping clients explore the benefits and risks of a certain choice along with available alternatives can help guide them to the decision that is right for them.

Instruction in Newborn Care Basics

Many postpartum doula clients report having very little newborn care experience. Some have never held a baby this young or small before. They expect you to have knowledge and expertise regarding all things relating to babies. This includes the safe handling of newborns, all modalities of infant feeding, best practices for diapering and bathing, various comforting and soothing techniques, and so much more. Your role as a doula is to listen to your clients, be certain that you understand their wishes, and provide a level of support that is compassionate and without bias.

Always be prepared to address your client's concerns in a professional and non-judgmental manner.

Holding and Handling Newborns

Never assume that your clients feel comfortable holding and handling a newborn. Many first time parents have never been exposed to, let alone held, a baby of this age before. It is normal for them to feel a bit apprehensive about this. Validate them and affirm for them that it's expected that they would feel this way. Assure them that you will support them in acclimating to this new experience.

Always support a newborn baby's head when holding and/or carrying them. As a professional doula, it is expected that you will model this for your clients.

Tips for holding and handling include:

- If the baby is positioned on your shoulder, you should always have one hand on the back of their head.
- When handing the baby to another adult, make sure that you have verbally affirmed with them that they have a secure hold of the baby before you let go.
- If carrying the baby up or down the stairs, you should not be holding anything but the baby.
- Never leave the baby unattended on any surface that they could roll or fall from, even if they have not begun rolling over yet.

If older siblings would like to hold the new baby, they should always do so supervised by another adult. Have the older child sit in a chair or couch, with some pillows for support, and then position their arms and hands in the proper place before settling the baby in their lap. Depending on the age of the older sibling, it may be best for an adult to always keep one hand on the baby. Stay next to the sibling so that the supervising adult can take the baby back as soon as the older child indicates they are ready.

Umbilical Cord Care

Following birth, the newborn's umbilical cord will be cut to separate the baby from the placenta. A small amount of this cord will remain attached to the newborn's abdomen until it has naturally dried out and fallen off on its own. This is the umbilical cord stump.

Care instructions include:

- Keep the umbilical stump clean
- Keep the umbilical stump dry by exposing it to air; do not use alcohol to dry it out
- Stick to sponge baths until it falls off
- Allow the umbilical stump to fall off on its own
- It is normal to see dried blood or a little "crust" around the cord site

Signs of infection may include the following and the client should be encouraged to call their pediatrician for any of the following:

- Redness or swelling in the cord area
- Continuous bleeding
- Yellow pus
- Foul smelling discharge

Diapering

Changing a newborn baby's diaper may be an area of newborn care that your clients have no prior experience with. While this is relatively easy to master, you can share some general care instructions and tips to make diapering that much more simple for new parents.

Help them feel prepared by creating diaper stations around the house, so there is always a convenient place nearby to change their baby's diaper. Supplies they may want to include at their changing stations:

- Changing pad
- Chux pads
- Diapers - always keep plenty stocked
- Baby wipes
- Wipe warmer
- A change of clothes in the proper size
- Burp cloths
- Diaper cream or ointment
- Diaper cream spatula

- Diaper pail

Instruct clients to always get prepared before removing a dirty diaper - having wipes out and a clean diaper unfolded and placed under the old one can prevent messy accidents that can occur when a baby is left un-diapered for too long.

Additional education surrounding diapering:

- Always wipe from "front to back," especially for baby girls to avoid introducing fecal matter and other bacteria into the genital area.
- Some newborn girls experience a "false period" - minor vaginal bleeding that is due to the rapid drop in hormones the baby was exposed to during birth - and will pass within 3-4 days.
- If the umbilical cord stump has not fallen off yet, fold down the top front of the diaper to prevent rubbing and irritation to that site.

Diaper Rash

It is not unusual for a baby to develop a diaper rash at some point during their pre-potty-trained period of life. For most babies, this is a mild irritation which, when carefully cared for, will pass relatively quickly.

Symptoms include:

- Pink or red patches on the skin around the groin or bottom or in the folds of the skin
- Itchy, tender skin around the diaper area
- Fussiness and crying during diaper changes

If you notice any of the above signs during diaper changes, be sure to:

- Change the diaper frequently
- Encourage the parents to use a gentle brand of baby wipe or a wet tissue
- Use a protective layer of diaper cream at each change
- Allow the baby's skin some time to air dry before applying the clean diaper

When diaper rash does not improve or it worsens over 3-4 days, the client should contact their pediatrician.

Signs and symptoms of worsening include:

- Open sores
- Peeling blisters
- Small, bright red spots (which could be a sign of a yeast or bacteria infection)
- The diaper rash seems painful
- The baby develops a fever

Cloth Diapering

Some parents prefer cloth diapers to disposable ones. This may be due to their cost effectiveness, environmental impact, baby's comfort, or personal philosophy.

If there's one thing to know about cloth diapers, it is that those who choose this method of diapering are often meticulous about their use and care. While washing routines may vary from client to client, there are a few general rules that should be followed:

- The diapers of exclusively breastfed babies can go right into the washing machine.
- Some families may prefer to rinse or dunk cloth diapers in the toilet before laundering.
- Diapers of an infant or child who is formula fed or eating solids should be rinsed or dunked in the toilet prior to being washed.
- When uncertain about laundry instructions for a particular diaper, refer to the manufacturer's recommendations.
- Fabric softener or detergents with fabric softeners cause a waxy build up that decreases their absorbency and should not be used.

If in doubt, always ask your clients to explain their washing and care routines for their cloth diapers to you.

Care of the Intact Penis

Care of the intact penis is relatively simple. Only clean what is seen. Begin at the base of the penis and wipe towards the tip using a clean, moist cloth or diaper wipe. Wipe the penis as you would a finger or any other body part to remove urine and any stool on or near the penis. Never retract the foreskin of an intact infant and encourage the client to make sure that the child's medical care providers and any caregivers know how to properly care for the intact penis.

Circumcision

Circumcision is a surgical procedure where the foreskin of the penis is removed. There are two methods to perform a circumcision. One is by making an incision and removing the foreskin surgically. The other, known as the Plastibell Technique, is done by using a plastic ring and tightly tying a string around the foreskin over the ring.

Cleaning, pain management, and general care are similar for both circumcision methods.

Normal recovery includes:

- Normal urination
- Appears to look red or swollen for the first day or two
- Has spots of blood or yellow crust at the tip
- Has blue-ish color (from bruising) where numbing medication may have been used

Home care:

- Petroleum jelly gauze may have been applied to the penis after surgery. Replace this gauze at diaper changes for the first 1-2 days as instructed.
- Put petroleum jelly on the penis at diaper changes for 3-5 days to prevent penis sticking to the diaper unless otherwise instructed. (Not necessary with a plastic ring.)
- Do not put any pressure on the penis.
- Change diapers right away and put clean diapers on loosely.
- If gauze sticks to the penis, apply warm water to loosen it.
- Clean the penis with a soft cloth or cotton ball and dry it gently.

Normal recovery does not include:

- Infant younger than 3 months old with a rectal temperature of 100.4° F.
- Infant older than 3 months old with a rectal temperature of 102° F.
- Blood is soaking the gauze.
- There is a foul odor or discharge coming from the penis.
- There is excessive redness or swelling.
- The skin of the penis is not healing by 7-10 days.
- The infant is unable to urinate.
- When a plastic ring has been used and it has not fallen off by the 8th day.

Bathing

Bath time is about more than a clean baby. Bathing a baby can also create an opportunity for bonding through touch. The three basic bathing techniques are sponge bathing, submersion bathing, and co-bathing.

Sponge bathing is the most common form of bathing for a newborn whose umbilical stump has not yet fallen off. Recommendations for not submerging a baby until its cord stump falls off varies by location.

Each family is given a set of recommendations upon discharge from the hospital for how to care for their newborn. For some families, exclusively following the information from the packet the hospital provides will be what is most comfortable for them. Other families may want to explore their options and make choices that suit them as individuals. As doulas, we support the client's choice and follow their lead.

Sponge Bathing

Supplies needed for sponge bathing:

- Infant tub or a clean, flat surface
- Baby soap/shampoo
- 2 soft washcloths
- Cotton balls
- Large, soft towel

When sponge bathing an infant it is important to remember:

- Gather all of the necessary supplies first.
- Put the tub on a flat, safe surface.
- Never walk away from the baby during the bath.
- Always keep one hand on the baby while bathing.

Sponge Bathing Process:

- Prepare water for bathing and set up the bath area.
- When sponge bathing a baby, it is preferable to not sit the baby in water as you bathe them, so prepare a basin or sink full of water to use for sponge bathing.
- If bathing the baby in a baby bathtub, settle the baby into the tub and cover the baby with a washcloth to keep them warm.
- For comfort, make a nest for the baby out of towels and keep the baby wrapped until bathing begins.
- Start at the top of the head and work your way down.
- Using a fresh cotton ball, moistened with plain, warm water, wash the baby's eyes/eyelids starting at the inside corner and wiping out towards the temple. Use a fresh cotton ball for each eye.
- Using a damp washcloth with mild soap, wash the baby's scalp.
- Use a clean, damp cloth to rinse. Cover each part of the baby you've bathed to keep them warm.
- Wash the baby's arms and armpits and use a clean, damp cloth to rinse.
- Wash the baby's legs and feet and use a clean, damp cloth to rinse.
- Support the baby with your hand and lean the baby forward to wash the baby's back and bottom. Use a damp cloth to rinse.
- Be sure to wash all folds and creases in the baby's neck, arms, and legs.
- Only clean what is seen; there is no need to use a Q-tip in baby's ears or nose and do not retract the intact male penis to clean beneath the foreskin.
- Wash the baby's genitals last.
- Once the baby is clean, wrap the baby in a clean towel to finish drying, then diaper and dress.

As a doula, you want to help build your client's confidence. Encourage them to sing and talk to their baby as well as make eye contact, soothing the baby as necessary during this bonding experience.

Submersion Bathing

Submersion bathing can happen in a few locations around the home. Some families prefer to put the infant bath tub across the sink or next to the sink on the counter top. Other families may choose to fill the sink with a foam bathing mat or soft towels. Sometimes a small basin is used and other families will place the infant tub within the bathtub.

Regardless of the location chosen, there are some basic bathing essentials to remember. Gather your supplies prior to beginning the bath (the same list of supplies from above can be used) and always keep one hand on the baby.

Submersion Bathing Process

- Begin by filling the tub, sink, or basin with as much water as you would like to submerge the baby in.
- Test the temperature of the water before submerging the baby to make sure it's not too hot or cold.
- Use one arm to support the baby's head, neck, and back and place him/her into the tub.
- Always keep one hand on the baby for safety.
- Begin by washing each eye with a moist cotton ball - one cotton ball for each eye and wipe from the inside corner out.
- Using a damp washcloth with mild soap, wash the baby's scalp; use the washcloth to rinse.
- Wash the baby's arms and armpits and rinse.
- Wash the baby's legs and feet and rinse.
- Support the baby with your hand and lean the baby forward to wash the baby's back and bottom, rinse.
- Be sure to wash all folds and creases in the baby's neck, arms, and legs.
- Only clean what is seen; there is no need to use a Q-tip in baby's ears or nose and do not retract the intact male penis to clean beneath the foreskin.
- Wash the baby's genitals last.
- Once the baby is clean, remove them from the water and wrap them in a clean, dry towel.
- Finish drying the baby, then diaper and dress.

Bonding experiences can be created through submersion bathing by talking or singing to the baby as you wash their body. Engage with the baby through eye contact and your voice, soothing the baby as necessary as you go along.

Some babies may enjoy the water and you can pour warm water over the baby's body to keep them warm as they enjoy laying in the water. You can also use a washcloth, wet with warm water, to lay on the baby's chest and belly, if exposed, to keep the baby warm. Periodically re-wet the washcloth with warm water and replace.

Co-Bathing

Co-bathing is an opportunity for bathing and bonding to occur simultaneously. While some families may wait until babies are a few months old before beginning to co-bathe, others will enjoy co-bathing from earlier on.

As with sponge bathing and submersion bathing, encourage your client to gather appropriate supplies before beginning. It may be helpful for you or the partner to pass the baby to the client once they are in the tub, and receive the baby once the bath is complete.

When co-bathing, the same process of washing the baby can be used as outlined above. When co-bathing, the parent typically has knees bent up and the baby lies in their lap.

Some will support the baby in the water with their hands while allowing the baby's body to be fully submerged. It is not uncommon to see babies who are supported in this position visibly relax into the water and their loving caregiver's hands.

Co-bathing can also be done once the baby is older by having one parent hand the baby to the other who is in the shower. Parents should be mindful that wet babies can be slippery, so some parents may not be comfortable with this option.

After the bath is complete, many parents choose to give the baby a soothing massage with their favorite moisturizer or baby-safe massage oil. This extends the bonding experience for the baby and parent as they enjoy the giving of massage and bonding through touch.

Taking the Baby's Temperature

While at one time, glass thermometers were the only option, today there are many options available for taking a baby's temperature. In the normal newborn, body temperature should range from approximately 97.8° to 98.8° F (rectal or axillary). If the baby has a temperature of 100.0° F or higher on two separate readings, encourage the client to contact the baby's medical provider.

How to Use

The following instructions pertain to digital thermometers.

Rectal

- Clean with rubbing alcohol or warm, soapy water.
- Coat the tip with petroleum jelly.
- Settle the baby onto their back and bend knees to chest.
- Turn the thermometer on.
- Insert the thermometer about 3/4 of an inch into the rectum.
- Hold the thermometer in place while supporting the baby's bottom.
- When the thermometer beeps, remove and read the temperature.
- Some babies may have a bowel movement when the thermometer is removed, so make sure to have a clean diaper or towel under the baby to catch any stool.
- Clean the thermometer again with alcohol or warm, soapy water, dry, and store.

Armpit or Axillary

- This method is recommended for babies 3 months or older.
- Remove the baby's shirt or onesie and make sure that the baby's armpit is dry.
- Turn on the thermometer.
- Insert bulb/tip of thermometer into the baby's armpit, making sure it is in full contact with the baby's skin.
- Hold the baby's arm snugly against his/her side.
- When the thermometer beeps, remove and read the temperature.

Digital Ear Thermometer

- Ear thermometers are not recommended for infants younger than 6 months.
- It is recommended that the client follow the specific instructions for their specific model.
- Ear thermometers are harder to use than other digital thermometers. It's suggested that you take both an ear reading and rectal reading at first to make sure that you are properly using the ear thermometer.

Temporal Artery Thermometer

- This method is recommended for babies 3 months or older.
- It is recommended that the client follow the manufacturer's instructions for their specific model.
- Temporal thermometers use infrared to read the temperature of the temporal artery through the skin in the forehead.

Medications

As a ProDoula trained Postpartum & Infant Care Doula, it is outside of your code of conduct to administer ANY kind of medication - orally or rectally - to a client or their baby. Anything that must be measured accurately according to prescribed dosage guidelines, such as reflux medication or vitamin D drops, shall not be administered by the doula. Topical creams, such as prescription diaper rash, do not fall under this prohibition since they do not have to be measured accurately and are not given orally.

* It is not appropriate for the ProDoula Postpartum & Infant Care doula to administer medications, herbal treatments, or homeopathic treatments to the infant. *

Notes:

Newborn and Infant Safety

As a new parent begins to learn their baby's needs and cries, it is likely that you will notice their confidence levels increasing. Each family is unique and it is expected that their choices and decisions will be equally as unique. As a professional doula you will affirm their decisions without judgment or bias. However, you must also be aware of important newborn and infant safety guidelines and be prepared to educate your clients, with compassion as these situations arise.

General Safety Tips and Guidelines

Water Safety - A baby, and even an older child, should never be left unattended in any amount of water, even an inch. Leaving a child unattended in the water is a drowning risk and an adult should be supervising baths and water play at all times. Even a quick trip to grab a towel out of the dryer or answer a knock at the door is an unacceptable amount of time to leave a baby alone.

Temperature - Because newborn babies can struggle to regulate their own body temperature, they can be susceptible to overheating. The room where the baby sleeps should be kept between 68°F and 72°F. Anything below 68°F can be too cold. Babies born prematurely, can have an especially hard time regulating their body temperatures. A temperature over 72°F can be too hot, causing a baby to overheat. Overheating can increase the risk of SIDS for babies.

Dressing - The general rule of thumb for newborns is to dress them in one layer more than an adult would feel comfortable in within the same environment. For example, if the adult is comfortable in shorts and a T-shirt, dress the newborn in a long sleeve shirt and pants. Be mindful of overheating when dressing babies - if you notice the baby sweating or red in the face, they are dressed too warmly. Babies should also never be dressed in any articles of clothing that present a strangulation or choking hazard - no loose strings or anything that could come off and get lodged in the baby's throat.

Babywearing - Depending on your client's parenting philosophies or lifestyle, they may find babywearing to be a convenient way to hold their baby. Many find it to be a wonderful bonding experience as well. or a special way to bond with their baby.

*A doula may wear a client's baby if they have discussed it with the parent and have been given their express permission.

The following is an acronym for babywearing safety:

- **T** - Tight - the carrier should always be tight and secure so there is no risk of falling
- **I** - In View - the baby's face should always be in view of the person wearing them
- **C** - Chin off Chest - the baby should always be in an upright position to make sure that their chin does not fall to their chest, which can close off airways
- **K** - Kiss (Close Enough) - the baby's head should be close enough to kiss for the person wearing the baby
- **S** - Supported Spine - the baby's spine should always be properly supported by the carrier and never twisted

Car Seat Safety - Babies and children should always be securely seated in an approved car seat for their age and weight when they travel in a vehicle. Unless you have taken a separate Car Seat and Safety Technician Certification, it is outside of your code of conduct as a Postpartum & Infant Care Doula to instruct your clients on car seat safety. You as the doula should never be the one to buckle a baby into their car seat or snap a car seat into the base inside the vehicle. That responsibility should always be on the parents.

Safe Sleep - This manual introduces infant sleep in more detail (see pg. 108), but a P&ICD should always be up to date on the AAP's Safe Sleep Guidelines. Most importantly, babies must always be placed on their backs, in their own flat, safe sleep surface, with nothing else present.

Older Siblings and Pets - If there are older siblings or pets in the house, the baby should never be left unsupervised with them. When engaging in tummy time or play on the floor, the supervising adult should be mindful to prevent pets or older siblings from falling or stepping on the baby. There should always be a safe space to set the baby down that is outside the reach of an older sibling or pet.

Notes:

Infant Care Red Flags

Fever

The most precise form of calculating an infant's temperature when the infant is under 3 months of age is with a digital thermometer via the rectum. When the parent takes the baby's temperature and it is 100.4 degrees fahrenheit (38 degrees celsius) or greater, they should be advised to contact the baby's healthcare provider.

Lethargy

A baby who is unable to be roused to feed, is unable to remain awake for feeds, and does not respond to sound or visual stimulus would be considered lethargic. This may be a sign of infection or low blood sugar. A baby who is displaying these signs should be referred to their healthcare provider for evaluation.

Inadequate Urination/Bowel Movements

A healthy newborn should have at least one wet diaper per day of life up to day five. So a baby who is one day old will have one wet diaper, a baby who is four days old should have four wet diapers, etc. After the 5th day it is expected that a baby will urinate 6 or more times per day. Urination is a sign of adequate hydration. When a parent is using disposable diapers it may be difficult to determine if the baby has urinated. Placing a small square of toilet paper or a folded tissue in the diaper and checking it every few hours can help a parent identify that the baby has urinated.

Rapid Breathing

While it is within the scope of normal for a newborn to have some irregularities in breathing, rapid breathing which is considered 60 or more breaths per minute or a pause in breathing for more than 10 seconds is a cause for concern. Whistling, grunting, or grunting while breathing, along with pulling in of the ribs (called retractions) are symptoms that should be brought to the attention of the baby's care provider immediately.

Discharge from Umbilical Stump

If the newborn has oozing, drainage, bleeding, or a foul odor coming from the umbilical cord stump this may be a sign of infection. These symptoms should be brought to the newborn's medical care provider immediately.

Jaundice & Bilirubin

Jaundice refers to the yellow color of an infant's skin and the whites of their eyes, caused by the breakdown of red blood cells which produce bilirubin. Bilirubin is processed by the infant's liver and when the bilirubin builds up faster than the baby's liver can process it through the body, jaundice is the result.

When severe jaundice is left untreated, complications such as brain damage, cerebral palsy, or deafness can occur. While rare, jaundice can be a sign of an underlying problem such as a thyroid condition, birth trauma, blood incompatibility between parent and baby, disease such as sickle cell anemia, or infection.

It is routine for infants to be screened for jaundice within a few days of birth. Babies who are not feeding well will often not be stooling well. The process of the elimination of bilirubin happens through the stool and this stalled process can create problems.

According to the American Academy of Pediatrics, bilirubin levels in a newborn should be under 5 mg/dl. Many newborns will have some kind of elevation of bilirubin as a result of the stress of birth. Phototherapy may be recommended and in severe cases of jaundice, an exchange transfusion may become necessary.

Jaundice is not a condition that should be taken lightly. Support the care plan laid out by the provider and refer the client back to the baby's care provider for any questions or concerns.

It is important that the doula does not underestimate how serious jaundice can become. Making promises about the baby's health or outcome is never appropriate.

Developmental Milestones

Developmental Milestones - Birth to 12 months	
Birth to 3 Months	<ul><li>**Hearing**<ul><li>Newborns who are hearing can hear sounds before birth. However, they are not yet able to identify sounds or words.</li><li>By one month of age babies begin to identify familiar sounds and may turn their head towards the source of the sound.</li><li>By three months of age babies may respond to familiar sounds with excitement or become quiet and focused on the sound of familiar voices.</li></ul></li><li>**Vision**<ul><li>Newborns who are sighted focus on things they can see at close distances, typically human faces.</li><li>By one month of age the baby will begin to demonstrate the ability to follow objects that pass in front of their face.</li><li>By two months of age the baby will begin to smile back at faces that are smiling at them.</li><li>By the end of the third month the baby will begin to search for and make eye contact.</li></ul></li><li>**Motor Skills**<ul><li>A newborn's movements will be jerky and uncoordinated.</li><li>By the second month most babies will begin to demonstrate the ability to control movements.<ul><li>Lifting their head</li><li>Supporting their own head for longer periods of time by month three</li></ul></li><li>By the end of the third month most babies can lift their head and chest with support from their elbows when placed on their tummy.</li><li>They will also begin to grasp toys/objects andbring them to their mouth.</li></ul></li></ul>

Developmental Milestones - Birth to 12 months	

Birth to 3 Months	• **Communication**
	  • For the first two months babies rely on crying to communicate their needs, and are responsive to body language, expressions from their caregivers.
	  • By the second month babies will begin to coo and may mimic vowel sounds spoken by caregivers.
	  • By the third month babies will begin to experiment with other sounds such as squeaking, growling, and blowing raspberries.
	    • They may also begin to smile at the sound of their caregiver's voice.

Developmental Milestones - Birth to 12 months	

4 to 6 Months	- **Vision**
	  - The baby begins to differentiate between shades of yellow, blue, and red.
	  - Items with high contrast and complex patterns will begin to hold their interest.
	  - They begin to focus on toys and find interest in looking at their own reflection.
	  - By the sixth month they may begin to follow objects that move beyond their immediate field of vision by turning their head.
	- **Motor Skills**
	  - The baby begins to kick and flail their arms and legs with intention.
	  - The baby begins rolling over.
	  - Most babies can raise their heads when lying face down.
	  - By the end of the sixth month they can maintain a sitting position when placed in one.
	- **Hand-Eye Coordination**
	  - The grasping skill continues to develop.
	  - Anything the baby can reach will likely be grasped and brought to their mouth.
	  - Babies begin to pull objects closer, utilizing a raking motion with their hands.
	- **Communication**
	  - Babies in this age range begin to put strings of sounds together and repeat sounds, ex. Ma-ma, da-da, ba-ba.
	  - Begin to distinguish emotions through tone of voice, for example a firm "no" may elicit sadness or fear.
	  - May begin to respond to their name.

Developmental Milestones - Birth to 12 months	
7 to 9 Months	• **Motor Skills** 　• May be able to roll over in both directions. 　• Most can sit unassisted but some may still need support. 　• May begin to rock on hands and knees, scoot, and begin crawling. 　• Some babies may begin to pull themselves into a standing position. • **Hand-Eye Coordination** 　• Most will be able to transfer an object from one hand to another. 　• Pincer grasp (thumb and finger grasping) begins to develop. 　　• This will begin to facilitate self feeding of soft foods • **Communication** 　• Continues to develop through gestures, sounds, and facial expressions. 　• The expression of sounds through creating chains of sounds continues to develop. 　• May accurately mimic specific sounds. • **Stranger Anxiety** 　• Fear or anxiety of strangers begins to develop at this time. • **Teething** 　• Begins to drool and chew on hands, objects, etc. with intention. 　• It may take several more months for teeth to erupt through the gums.

Developmental Milestones - Birth to 12 months	

10 to 12 Months	- **Motor Skills**
	  - Most babies can get into a sitting position without assistance and pull themselves into a standing position.
	  - Many will begin to walk while holding on to stable mobjects.
	  - By 12 months many will begin to take first steps without support.
	- **Hand-Eye Coordination**
	  - Pincer grasp is continuing to develop and most babies can self feed finger foods.
	  - Some babies will begin to use self feeding tools.
	  - Growing interest in banging objects together, may place objects in a container and remove.
	- **Communication**
	  - Begin to respond to simple verbal requests.
	  - May begin to utilize gestures such as waving and shaking or nodding head in response to yes or no.
	  - Expansion of vocabulary by using more words and identifying objects when asked, i.e., "Where is the ball?"
	- **Development of Cognitive Skills**
	  - Begins to understand that objects still exist even when not in view, for example peek-a-boo, removing a blanket covering an object below.
	  - Begins to imitate actions of others, waving, playing on a phone, pushing buttons on a remote, etc.

Source: Mayo Clinic

Pediatrician Visits/Vaccine Schedule

	Pediatrician Visits from Birth to Twelve Months	
Birth	At birth the baby will receive a head to toe evaluation by a member of the medical team. The location of the birth will determine which provider will complete the newborn exam. During this exam the provider is assessing: • Normal body functions such as breathing, reflexes, muscle tone, alertness and hip flexibility. • The baby will be weighed and their length will be measured. • Head and chest circumference will be measured. • A head-to-toe exam to assess ears, eyes, mouth, skin, heart and lungs, abdomen, hips and legs, and genitalia. • Hearing screening. • Newborn metabolic screening.	Vaccinations: • VitK • HepB before discharge
3-7 Days	• The baby will be weighed and their length will be measured. • Head circumference will be measured. • A head-to-toe exam to assess ears, eyes, mouth, skin, heart and lungs, abdomen, hips and legs, and genitalia. • Hearing screening - if not completed after birth. • Newborn metabolic screening - if not completed after birth.	• HepB if not given before discharge

1 Month	• The baby will be weighed and their length will be measured. • Head circumference will be measured. • A head-to-toe exam to assess ears, eyes, mouth, skin, heart and lungs, abdomen, hips and legs, and genitalia.	• First dose of HepB if not given before discharge • Second dose of HepB

Pediatrician Visits from Birth to Twelve Months		
2 Months	• The baby will be weighed and their length will be measured. • Head circumference will be measured. • A head-to-toe exam to assess ears, eyes, mouth, skin, heart and lungs, abdomen, hips and legs, and genitalia.	• Second dose of HepB if first dose was given at 1 month First dose of: • RV • DTaP • HiB • PCV • IPV
4 Months	• The baby will be weighed and their length will be measured. • Head circumference will be measured. • A head-to-toe exam to assess ears, eyes, mouth, skin, heart and lungs, abdomen, hips and legs, and genitalia.	Second dose of: • RV • DTaP • Hib • PCV • IPV

6 Months	• The baby will be weighed and their length will be measured.
	• Head circumference will be measured.
	• A head-to-toe exam to assess ears, eyes, mouth, skin, heart and lungs, abdomen, hips and legs, and genitalia.
	• They may also receive:
	  • Lead screening
	  • Tuberculosis testing
	  • Oral exam to check any new teeth
		Third dose of:
		• DTaP
		• Hib
		• PCV

9 Months	• The baby will be weighed and their length will be measured. • Head circumference will be measured. • A head-to-toe exam to assess ears, eyes, mouth, skin, heart and lungs, abdomen, hips and legs, and genitalia. • Formal developmental screening.	Fourth dose of: • HepB Possible third dose of: • IPV
12 Months	• The baby will be weighed and their length will be measured. • Head circumference will be measured. • A head-to-toe exam to assess ears, eyes, mouth, skin, heart and lungs, abdomen, hips and legs, and genitalia.	Fourth dose of: • PCV First dose of: • MMR • VAR • HepA

Source: American Academy of Pediatrics & Centers for Disease Control

Vaccine Key:

Abbreviation	Vaccine Name
VitK	Vitamin K
HepB	Hepatitis B
DTaP	Diphtheria, tetanus, & acellular pertussis
HiB	Haemophilus influenzae type b
PCV	Pneumococcal conjugate
IPV	Inactivated poliovirus
RV	Rotavirus

RSV	Respiratory syncytial virus
MMR	Measles, mumps, rubella
HepA	Hepatitis A
VAR	Varicella

When a parent has a concern about their baby's development or what to expect at pediatrician visits, the doulas role is to provide educational support and help them become familiar with what they can expect. Doulas do not give medical advice or diagnose developmental issues. Doulas provide resources, education, and refer the client back to the baby's provider for evaluation and any respective diagnosis and treatment.

Vaccines

Discussions surrounding routine childhood vaccinations can become controversial in parenting circles. Many parents choose to follow the CDC's recommended vaccination schedule (see below), but it is important to note that some families may choose a modified schedule or elect not to vaccinate at all.
While in many locations, vaccinations are mandatory in order to attend public school, exemptions may exist that allow a child who has not been vaccinated access to a public education. These exemptions are medical, religious, and philosophical in nature and may not be recognized by some states or provinces.

The Center for Disease Control (CDC) recommendation for childhood vaccinations for the United States can be found here:
https://www.cdc.gov/vaccines/schedules/hcp/imz/child-adolescent.html

Parents can speak to their pediatricians about alternatives as well.

Caring for Premature Babies/Medically Fragile Babies

From the positive pregnancy test, the expecting parents begin to imagine what life with their new baby will be like. When they envision meeting their baby, it is typically a joyous, exciting meeting, involving a healthy newborn. If the reality of that first meeting involves a preterm infant or a medically fragile baby, this can be a drastic departure from what the parents prepared for.

As always, your role as a Postpartum & Infant Care Doula will encompass not just educational and physical support, but emotional support as well. Clients with a preterm or medically fragile baby may need that emotional support the most.

Premature Babies

A birth is considered "preterm" when a baby is born before 37 weeks of pregnancy. Other categories of preterm birth include:

- Late preterm (34-36 weeks)
- Moderately preterm (32-34 weeks)
- Very preterm (less than 32 weeks)
- Extremely preterm (less than 25 weeks)

Adjusted Age

A premature baby's age is calculated in two ways.

Chronological Age - the age of the baby from the date of birth

Adjusted Age - the age of the baby based on their due date

For example, if a baby who was born 2 months premature is 6 months old, their adjusted age is 4 months old. This is what a baby's growth and development are based on. Most premature babies catch up on growth and development by 2 to 2.5 years of age.

Things to be aware of:

- Some premature babies are multiples and may not come home together.
- Premature babies may be more sensitive to touch, light, and sudden noise. Over-stimulation is not uncommon.
- Premature babies may sleep more and have a harder time with feeding.
- It is likely that they will be on a strict schedule during their time in the NICU and many parents find it essential to maintain this schedule once their baby/ies is/are home.
- Premature babies are more susceptible to illness. Hand washing is essential.
- Parents of premature babies are at higher risk of developing a postpartum mood or anxiety disorder.

The doula's role:

- Support the parents in getting as much sleep as possible.
- If desired, help with creating a schedule for the parents, including NICU visits, pumping, sleeping, and eating.
- Keep easy to grab snacks and meals in small containers stored in the refrigerator for when parents are home between NICU visits or to have available for them to grab on the go.
- Help with older kids.
- Be emotionally available to provide a shoulder to cry on or an ear for unbiased, non-judgmental listening.

Multiples

Managing Multiples

When a family welcomes multiples, the workload can multiply as well. Fortunately, there are many approaches to caring for multiples that will allow the family to streamline care and make caring for two or more babies more manageable.

As you begin working with families, assess their philosophies and preferences around parenting and raising their children.

For example:

• Attachment parenting	• Scheduled parenting
• Breastfeeding	• Formula feeding
• Cloth diapering	• Sleeping preferences

Your role as a doula is to help support the family in their decisions regarding their children. Putting multiples on the same schedule can afford the family more rest. However, parenting decisions are ultimately for the parents to make and for you to support.

The following are areas that you may want to explore, practice, and become educated on when working with multiples.

For many families of multiples, scheduling may become a necessary part of their parenting plans. Scheduling also allows parents to optimize the time available to tend to their personal needs, such as self care and sleep.

Often when there is more than one baby it is hard to track when the baby pooped, fed, etc. There are many online tracking apps available for families to use, such as:

- **Baby Connect** - Available across multiple mobile operating systems. Tracks: feeding, diapers, sleep, temperature, medication, and much more.
- **Total Baby** - Available for iOS and Google Play. Tracks: feeding, diapers, sleep, etc. Features dual timers that can be used for each child. Can compare today to previous days.
- **Huckleberry** - Available for Apple and Android devices. Tracks: feeding, diapers, sleeps; compares daily schedules and long-term

patterns.

Many families may find it helpful to utilize a chart that records the times each baby was fed, how much they took, and when they had dirty diapers. Families whose babies were in the NICU may come home with this type of system in place. Depending on the family's needs and the personality style of the parents, this may be a useful tool to introduce to the family as part of your services.

When creating charts to track feeding and diapering or other baby care tasks, it is often helpful to color code each baby, especially in the early days when input or output may need to be tracked carefully to ensure the baby is feeding and gaining adequately.

Color coding can also be incorporated by painting one of the baby's toenails a certain color in the case of identical twins, or assigning a certain color bottle or color of clothing to each baby for identification purposes.

Sample Twins Care Chart

Baby A		Baby B	
Feed Time:	12:32PM	Feed Time:	12:35PM
Ounces:	1.5	Ounces:	2
Diaper Change Time:	12:50PM	Diaper Change Time:	1:10PM
Wet/Soiled:	Wet	Wet/Soiled:	Wet & Soiled

It is important to remember that while multiples may have been born on the same day, they are still individuals. Each baby may develop at different rates, have differing personalities, may hit milestones at different times, and they may or may not have different feeding and diapering patterns. It can become especially difficult for parents to remember not to compare one baby to the other(s). Help them to remember that each baby is an individual and to celebrate their differences.

Holding Multiples

Another aspect of navigating the care of multiples is learning how to hold more than one baby at a time when necessary. It is important to assess the parent's comfort level with having both babies held by the same person at the same time. Some families may prefer that only one baby be held while moving from place to place. The client's home will influence your strategies around moving the babies from room-to-room or floor-to-floor.

Practicing with dolls at home can be helpful in learning how to pick up and hold two babies at once. It is important that when demonstrating or teaching parents how to hold more than one baby that you do so with confidence.

When you are one person caring for two babies, it is essential that you set up your space in order to have the items necessary to care for the babies close at hand. For example: diapers, wipes, change of clothes, etc.

Breastfeeding Multiples

When working with a client who wishes to breastfeed multiples, it is important to learn their goals for breastfeeding. Possible discussion questions may include:

- What are your breastfeeding goals?
- Short term/long term?
- Exclusive breastfeeding/supplementation?
- Feeding on demand/feeding on a schedule?
- Are you interested in learning to nurse both babies at the same time?
- What type of support system do you have in place for breastfeeding?
- How can I help you best?

While not all breastfeeding parents will desire to feed the babies simultaneously, for many it may be one of their breastfeeding goals. As a doula, part of your role may be to serve as a set of extra hands as your client begins their breastfeeding journey.

As a Postpartum & Infant Care Doula, it is not expected that you will have all the answers to your client's breastfeeding questions. However, it is important that you have identified resources to direct your client to when their questions or needs go beyond your abilities.

Examples of helpful resources include:

- La Leche League Meetings
- Multiples Support Group

- Breastfeeding Support Groups
- International Board Certified Lactation Consultant (IBCLC)

Safe Sleep for Multiples

According to the American Academy of Pediatrics, multiples should sleep on their own safe sleep surface and not bed-share with siblings. Whether or not multiples sleep together is for the parents to decide. As doulas, we can encourage safe sleep habits with our clients, while offering non-judgmental support.

Growth Charts

It is not uncommon for parents to become hyper-focused on their baby's growth. Some believe that they must be at the top of the growth curve in order to be healthy. Others feel that if their baby is towards the bottom of the growth curve that they may not be growing well.

It is important for doulas to understand that growth is individual and depends on genetic factors as well. A baby whose parents are of short stature may have consistent and appropriate growth but land on the bottom of the growth curve. This is completely normal.

Providers are looking for consistent growth from one entry to the next. A baby who is growing well and then begins to fall off the growth curve would prompt the provider to take a closer look at the baby's overall health and/or feeding patterns to look for any areas of concern.

The expected growth curve for the newborn is to return to birth weight by two weeks after birth.

Providers also take into account the baby's overall development. For example, a baby who was following the expected growth curve over the course of the first 6 months who doesn't gain as much weight as expected between visits may not have a health concern. It may be that the baby has become mobile, crawling for example, and this increased activity may slow or pause their weight gain.

Growth charts are a tool to look at the bigger picture to monitor growth over time.

The World Health Organization (WHO) has developed growth standards to monitor the growth of infants and children from birth to age two. The Centers for Disease Control (CDC) recommends that health providers who care for infants and children utilize these standards to track growth.

The most recent international standards were released in 2006 and were established from growth patterns among children whose diets were primarily breastmilk for at least 4 months and who were still breastfeeding at 12 months.

The CDC growth charts may not represent the ideal growth patterns for all infants from birth to age two. The WHO charts establish the standards for how children should grow under optimal living and nutritional conditions.

The WHO charts are broken down into two sets.

Boys Weight for Length Percentiles and Head Circumference for Age Percentiles	Boys Length for Age Percentiles and Weight for Age Percentiles
Girls Weight for Length Percentiles and Head Circumference for Age Percentiles	Girls Length for Age Percentiles and Weight for Age Percentiles

After the age of two, CDC growth charts can be used from age 2-19 years old.

As a doula, it is important to remember that our clients sometimes place a heavy emphasis on where their baby is on the growth chart. It can be stressful for the client if their baby is measuring low or near the bottom. Encourage your client to discuss any concerns they have with their healthcare provider and to determine what chart - the WHO or CDC - their provider is using. You can also play an important role by providing a non-judgmental, listening ear and affirming their feelings.

Navigating What We Don't Know

It is easy to feel overwhelmed with all the new information you have learned during your workshop. As a result, you may put a lot of pressure on yourself to remember every single detail.

The families who hire us may be looking to us for answers, but it is important to remember that we will never have all of the answers. What we do have is the ability to find the information they are seeking and communicate it to our clients in a style they will best receive.

As a Postpartum & Infant Care Doula it is appropriate to let your client know when you don't have the answer to their specific question, but you do have the ability to find it quickly. Set a deadline for when you will reach out to them with the requested information and make sure that you follow through accordingly.

Every opportunity that you take to research and find the information that your client is seeking is a chance for you to learn, grow, and increase your knowledge base. Consider creating a resource guide for yourself to refer back to for easy reference.

Remember, the ProDoula Training & Development Team as well as the Home Office are here to support you.

Obtain a Broad Sense of Knowledge

We are living in a rapidly changing world. Changes in technology and science are touching every field of study, so general knowledge is difficult to obtain. By choosing to be a doula you are already in a way picking your specialty, but within this field there exists a broad range of subjects.

As a doula you will provide physical, emotional, and informational support to the client during the postpartum period. This means you must continuously build your level of knowledge in the areas where clients will expect your support.

Your personal experience, combined with this certification course, is a good start, but you are expected to actively research areas where change is sure to happen, such as products, equipment, trends, philosophies, procedures, and more. The Internet is a vast source of information and we encourage you to use it in your personal development.

Common Baby Products

It is not uncommon to find a wide variety of baby products in a client's home. As Postpartum & Infant Care Doulas, it is recommended that you be up-to-date on baby products and have a general understanding of their purpose.

Monitors - There are several different types of monitors available.

- Audio Only: Allows the baby to be heard if left alone in a room.
- Video: Allows the baby to be seen and heard if left alone in a room. Some video monitors also have the ability to talk to the baby through them, as well as give a reading on the room temperature.
- Movement Monitor: These units are designed to alert the caregiver if movement is not detected for a pre-set period of time or if movements are irregular. It should be noted that these monitors are not intended to prevent SIDS.

Bottle Warmers - A simple, convenient, and safe option when it comes to heating breastmilk or formula, especially when compared to warming it in a bowl of hot water or running it under the tap.

Sterilizer - Used to sterilize bottles, nipples, pacifiers, and pump parts; could be a stand alone machine or microwaveable steam bags.

Swings - Can be used as a tool to help calm a fussy baby. Swings can also be a convenient, safe space to sit the baby so parents can take on necessary tasks such as making dinner, folding laundry, or other household or personal care tasks that can be completed while the parent is present. However, babies should never be left sleeping in a swing that is inclined due to the risks of positional asphyxiation.

Pack 'n Play: A portable crib and changing area.

Bouncy Seat: A portable seat to place the baby in that gently bounces up and down as the baby moves their legs; some have a vibration setting and play music.

Activity Mat: A soft place to lay the baby down or practice tummy time; they often have toys hanging from them for the baby to look at.

Product Safety Recalls

There are a wide variety of baby products on the market today; from feeding to sleeping to diapering to playtime, there is always something available to fit the parents' needs. But just because a product is sold in stores does not always mean that it is safe.

As a Postpartum & Infant Care Doula, one of your responsibilities is to stay up to date on consumer product safety and safety recalls that can affect your clients and their babies. According to the Consumer Product Safety Commission, retailers and manufacturers within the United States are required to recall a product if it fails to comply with a safety rule or regulation, could create a substantial hazard, or creates an unreasonable risk of serious injury or death. Unfortunately, many recalls are triggered after a baby has already been injured by a product sold in stores. It's quite possible that your clients could have also purchased this recalled product but be unaware of the safety risks it poses.

Following major baby product companies on social media, staying abreast of news stories, and setting up Google Safety alerts are all ways that you can monitor product safety recalls and stay up to date on the latest developments. You can set up a Google Alert by going to www.google.com/alerts and entering the topic you would like to receive alerts about. Think of a wide variety of keywords that could be pertinent here and set those as alerts. You will receive an email notification any time Google finds a safety alert on that subject.

The Tertiary Focus

The client's physical and emotional transition to parenthood along with their newborn's adjustment to life outside the womb will always be your top priorities as a Postpartum & Infant Care Doula. Once those needs are met, your tertiary focus will be on tasks related to the household - this could be helping with older sibling adjustment, preparing meals and snacks to feed the family, or light household chores that have been piling up. Remember, by taking care of these things for your client you are allowing them more time to focus on their physical and emotional recovery and bonding time with their new baby.

Sibling Care

The role of the doula involves supporting the entire family, not just the newly delivered parent and baby. Siblings are an important part of the family and, along with everyone else, the sibling is going through an adjustment period.

When interviewing with the client, ask about the siblings and their plans for the adjustment of the existing children. Ask the client how you can help. When you arrive at the home each day, be sure to address the sibling by bending down to their eye level to greet them for a couple of minutes prior to starting your activities with the baby, client, or household.

Part of your role as a doula is to engage the older siblings while the client is resting or feeding the baby. To help the sibling adjust if they show interest, you can encourage them to help you with helping the family.

- Fold or bring the diaper to you
- Help stock the baby's dressing table with diapers and supplies
- Help dress, burp, and feed the baby

You can also:

- Teach them to smile and talk to the baby, especially when the baby is fussy. Be sure to let the older child know that you are aware that the baby is enjoying the interaction.
- Help them hold the baby with supervision.
- Share some (but not all) toys with the baby - let the older child keep the toys that are very special to him or her.
- Create a feeding toy box – special toys the child can only play with

while the client is feeding the baby.

Sometimes the client will want you to take care of the older child's needs and sometimes they will want you to care for the baby so that they can enjoy an activity with the other child.

When possible, maintain the older child's normal routines.

Supporting the Client:

D	Ask, "What have you decided you will do about this (any situation)?"
I	"I will be by your side through this whole thing, you can count on my support."
S	Ask, "Have you talked to your partner about this? Or other family members that you trust?"
C	"I am happy to do some research on this for you if you'd like?"

D	I	S	C
Dominant	Inspirational	Supportive	Cautious
Driven	Influential	Submissive	Competent
Demanding	Induces emotion	Stable	Calculating
Determined	Impressive	Security minded	Concerned
Decisive	Interactive	Sentimental	Compliant
Delegates	Interested in people	Safe	Contemplative

Meal Preparation

Nutrition and hydration are two factors that are crucial to a healthy recovery from birth. If the client is breast or chest feeding, they must take in enough calories and nutrients to support the baby's growth as well as their own energy levels. Ideally, the client will have consulted with their doctor to determine a healthy caloric intake and prepared a postpartum meal plan.

In most cases, couples will not have thought about this in advance. As a result, part of your role as a Postpartum & Infant Care Doula is to aid the client by reminding them to eat and drink. While you are in the home you will want to make sure that their water glass is full and remind them to drink often. This is something that a newly delivered parent can easily neglect.

Snacks

New parents are often fatigued when acclimating to their baby's eating and sleeping schedule. Instead of the client eating three large meals per day, encourage them to eat small meals more often throughout the day to help maintain their energy level.

Light, nutritional, easily accessible foods are important and helpful to have prepared ahead of time. During your shift, ask if you can prepare some easily accessible snacks to leave in the refrigerator. Be sure that the snacks are ready-to-eat and do not require additional preparation once you leave the home.

Examples:

- Raw vegetables or cut fruit or grapes free of stems, washed and put in plastic containers
- Cut up a block of cheese and store in the fridge
- Hard boiled eggs, peeled
- Cold sandwiches cut in half, wrapped individually and labeled

Meals

Initially, friends and family may drop off or have food delivered to the new family, but that normally ends within the first week. This usually means take-out or leftovers for the new family which does not always provide the most nutritional benefits. Preparing meals for your clients is a greatly appreciated service. You don't have to be a great chef, but you should have a few meals in your repertoire.

Examples:

- Roast chicken with pasta and vegetables
- A pot of soup or hearty stew
- Meatloaf with mashed potatoes and green beans
- Pasta with vegetables

Household Support

In many cultures outside of the United States, the expectation is that the birthing person will have plenty of opportunities to rest and recover, while other people maintain the household for them. In China, the birthing person is allowed to rest for 30 days after giving birth. In India, postpartum confinement lasts up to 40 days. In Mayan Indian culture in Mexico, a new parent and infant must remain inside for 7 days.

In the US, however, there is no guaranteed parental leave, friends and family can live far apart, and societal pressures can make it difficult for newly delivered parents to just rest.

Doing what we can to help a client feel relaxed and comfortable while they are recovering from giving birth, learning to feed their newborn, and bonding with the baby should be considered an honor, not a chore. During this time, they may have family and friends coming to the house to help, but they will quickly find that visitors are there to hold the baby and not wash the dishes.

Part of your role in the home is to help the client with light housework and laundry. How much or how little you do will depend on both the client and you. Remember that with different personality types you will find different levels of "personal space."

For the most part, light housework will include:

- Sweeping/vacuuming
- Washing dishes
- Cleaning countertops
- Picking up toys
- Laundry

Light housework does NOT normally include:

- Washing floors
- Cleaning bathrooms
- Cleaning litter boxes
- Heavy, weekly cleaning

The best approach is to ask the client, but they may be so tired that they have not had time to think about it. While the client is resting and the baby is sleeping, take the initiative and find things to pick up and clean.

Supporting the Client:

D	Be direct. Ask how they are feeling both physically and emotionally.
I	Remind the client that you are there for them and they can share anything with you. Ask how they have been feeling emotionally.
S	Praise their commitment to their family and ask if there is anything upsetting them.
C	Suggest they keep a journal regarding their recovery and their feelings. Let them know you have the best resources available for anything they may need.

D	I	S	C
Dominant	Inspirational	Supportive	Cautious
Driven	Influential	Submissive	Competent
Demanding	Induces emotion	Stable	Calculating
Determined	Impressive	Security minded	Concerned
Decisive	Interactive	Sentimental	Compliant
Delegates	Interested in people	Safe	Contemplative

Notes:

Parenting Philosophies

For new parents, identifying their own parenting philosophy based on what feels right to them and having someone support and validate them is an empowering step.

Attachment Parenting Principles

The belief that:

- Breastfeeding is the optimal way to satisfy an infant's nutritional and emotional needs.
- Touch meets a baby's needs for physical contact, affection, security, stimulation, and movement.
- Skin-to-skin contact is especially important and is often facilitated through breastfeeding, bathing, and massage.
- Keeping the baby close through carrying or babywearing meets the baby's need for touch.

Dr. Sears's Principles

Dr. William Sears is a well-known pediatrician and the author or coauthor of more than 30 parenting books. While the practices behind this parenting philosophy have been in existence since the dawn of man, and ingrained among numerous cultures, Dr. Sears has become recognized in recent society for organizing these practices under the heading of "Attachment Parenting." He is the author of:

The 7 Bs of Attachment Parenting:

1. Birth bonding
2. Breastfeeding
3. Babywearing
4. Bedding close to baby
5. Belief in the language value of the baby's cry
6. Beware of baby trainers
7. Balance

Studies that focus on attachment parenting are typically based on anthropological or cross-cultural studies and tend to be naturalistic in nature. It is important to contextualize these sources and recognize that their effects are often inferred.

A paper in the Turkish Archives of Pediatrics in 2019 explored the importance and impact of attachment parenting on infant development and outlined the practices that demonstrated the most impact.

> *"The following behaviors support and improve attachment: pacifying, cuddling and patting the baby, calling the baby with their name or gender (my boy/my girl), talking with the baby, establishing eye-to-eye contact, nursing and using the appropriate nutrition method, if nursing is not possible. Skin contact leads to increased oxytocin secretion in the [parent] in addition to triggering sensory stimuli. With increased oxytocin, the [birth parent] calms down and [their] social sensitivity increases. This may improve parental attitudes and support attachment. It has been observed that physical and emotional relations were supported and communication was improved with [birth parents] who used the kangaroo method when cuddling their babies. It is important to share the same room in the postnatal period. In fact, each time the [birth parent] and baby separate, a psychological tension develops for both sides. The [birth parent] and baby should stay in the same room unless a medical necessity exists. With this approach, early contact can be provided, milk production increases, and the [birth parent's] self-confidence for more efficient nursing may increase.*

Source: The importance of attachment in infant and influencing factors. Turk Pediatri Ars. 2019 Jul 11

Scheduled Parenting Principles

Some common beliefs around scheduled parenting include:

- Creating schedules around feedings and sleep.
- The belief that when the baby is on a predictable schedule, the parents quickly feel more confident.
- The benefits of scheduled parenting help maintain normalcy and structure in the day-to-day lives of busy parents.

Dr. Karp's Principles

Dr. Harvey Karp is a pediatrician known for the techniques he developed for calming infants. He has written two popular books, The Happiest Baby on the Block and The Happiest Toddler on the Block.

According to Dr. Karp, human babies are born less developed than other mammals, and parents should treat the infant's first three months of life as a fourth trimester.

This means:

- Swaddling to recreate the space in the womb.
- Side/Stomach position.
- Shushing as if making the noise the baby hears in the womb.
- Swinging/Swaying to create a gentle and constant jiggling motion.
- Sucking on pacifiers or at the breast.

In 2019 a randomized controlled study was published in the Japan Journal of Nursing Science that examined the results of teaching new parents 4 of the 5 Ss of soothing:

> "After the teaching of the 4S soothing techniques had been conducted, it was determined that the mean frequency of waking at night, the mean frequency of daily feeding, and the mean daily crying duration of the infants in the [intervention group] was statistically significantly lower in all follow-ups, compared to the infants in the [control group]. In weeks 7 and 11 after the intervention, the mean daily sleep duration of the infants in the [intervention group] was found to be statistically significantly higher, compared to the infants in the [control group]."

For the purpose of this study sucking was not included as one of the soothing techniques.

Source: Effect of soothing techniques on infants' self-regulation behaviors (sleeping, crying, feeding): A randomized controlled study, Renginar Öztürk Dönme | 06 February 2019

Attachment Parenting on a Schedule

Many families identify with a little bit from both of these parenting philosophies.

- Perhaps they desire to breastfeed exclusively, but want to do it on a predictable schedule.
- Maybe they want to hold or wear their baby for comfort, but put them down to sleep.
- They may prefer a medical approach to birth, but be fiercely aligned to other aspects of attachment parenting.

As the doula, we help our clients have the best of every world. The client chooses what resonates best for them and the doula helps them create and initiate a strategy that aligns with their wishes.

Comfort & Soothing

The choices our clients make in regards to comfort and soothing are closely linked to their parenting philosophies. Make sure that you are in tune with your client's philosophies so that you can assist them in these areas and set them up for success when it comes to meeting their parenting goals.

For instance, if you know your client wants to be able to have their baby sleep swaddled in their crib for naps during the day, it will not be helpful for this client if you wear their baby in a carrier during your entire shift.

As postpartum doulas it is important to be aware of the risks of sleep deprivation on adults, especially those who are caring for newborn babies. In 2017, 91,000 police-reported crashes involved drowsy drivers. According to the National Highway Traffic Safety Administration the number of fatalities involving drowsy drivers was 684 or 1.6 percent of total fatalities in 2021. Which represents an 8.2 percent increase from 632 in 2020. The National Sleep Foundation states that being awake for 24 hours impairs cognitive and motor function equal to a blood alcohol level of .10, which is considered legally drunk.

The recommendation to take the baby for a car ride to help them sleep is common. However, desperate parents who are in need of sleep themselves put not only their own family at risk but others who share the road with them as well. As doulas it is important to underscore that it is okay to walk away from a crying baby to collect and regroup.

For many clients, prioritizing their sleep will be one of their main goals. Teaching them to comfort and soothe their babies will help them optimize their self care.

Swaddling

Swaddling a baby is one of the longest used infant care techniques, spanning many cultures and generations, and has long been a prominent part of routine infant care.

Benefits (tend to wear off by 3 to 4 months of age):

- Swaddled babies may wake up less often during sleep, startle less, and tend to sleep longer.

- Swaddling does not affect the baby's ability to wake themselves up when hungry or when they have another need.
- In babies younger than 2 months of age, research has shown that swaddling may also decrease crying.

Risks:

- Developmental dysplasia of the hip (a slightly dislocated hip joint) if the infant is swaddled for prolonged periods with straight legs.
- Swaddling may increase the risk of SIDS if the baby is placed on their side or their stomach while swaddled.
- Loose blankets may cover the baby's head.
- Too tight of a swaddle may make breathing more difficult.

Alternatives:

- Wearing baby
- Holding baby
- Not swaddling baby

There are several different ways to swaddle a baby:

- V-neck swaddle with receiving blanket
- Arm wrap swaddle
- Arms only swaddle
- Use of swaddle blankets
    - Miracle blanket
    - Aden and Anais Classic Muslin Swaddle Blankets
    - Woombie Swaddling Blankets
    - Love to Dream Swaddling Blankets
    - Summer Infant SwaddleMe Swaddling Blankets
- Arms out - this is helpful when it is time to begin the transition from swaddling to a sleep sack when baby is starting to learn to roll

Pacifier Use

Many babies have an insatiable need to suck. Research has overwhelmingly shown that sucking, whether it is for nutrition or comfort, helps the baby to calm themselves and to gain control when feeling stressed.

Benefits:

- Reduced risk of SIDS up through one year of age (routine use reduces risk by 15%-30%, use at the "big sleep" cuts SIDS risk in half)
- Calms babies
- Slows their pulse
- Decreases crying
- Increases their attentiveness
- For premature babies, comfort sucking has been linked to shorter NICU stays
- Benefits are greatest leading up to 6 months of age

Risks:

- After 6 months of age, slight increase in risk of ear infection
- After 18 months to 2 years of age, increase in risk of dental/orthodontic problems with more than 4 to 6 hours of daily sucking

Alternatives:

- Finger
- Bring baby to the breast
- Thumb or hand sucking

Pacifiers and Breastfeeding

Pacifiers may interfere with breastfeeding when they are used to replace a feed or when they are used to postpone a feeding. This may result in the reduction of milk production by reducing breast stimulation. There is little evidence that shows using a pacifier between feedings will interfere with breastfeeding. In fact, some research has shown pacifier use may support breastfeeding as the breastfeeding parent does not feel as if they are the only one who is able to calm the baby through sucking.

Self Soothing

Many families want their baby to learn how to fall asleep on their own. Helping a baby to learn how to do this from an early age helps to set the foundation for the baby being able to sleep through the night once they are developmentally ready. It also may prevent parents from feeling like they have to allow their baby to cry it out in order for them to learn how to self-soothe.

Teaching a Baby to Self-Soothe:

- Watch for signs that the baby is tired
- Gazing off, looks away, looks through you (zoning out)
- Calmer/less active
- Sucks slower
- Redness around the eyes
- Droopy eyelids
- Signs the baby may be overtired:
    - Crankiness
    - Flailing arms and legs
    - Crying uncontrollably
- When the baby shows signs of being tired, but not overtired, begin getting the baby ready for nap or bedtime
- Swaddle baby
- You may rock the baby until they look like they're about to fall asleep but are still awake
- Put the baby down on a safe sleep surface while awake and pat their chest or "shhh" them until they fall asleep; eventually, you'll be able to lay baby down awake and they will fall asleep on their own
- It's okay to allow the baby a minute of mild fussing, some babies just need a moment to adjust to something different; if baby becomes upset, pick the baby up and repeat the process as needed
- Suggesting that baby cry it out is not an appropriate recommendation as a doula

Swinging, Bouncing, and Rocking

As discussed previously, swinging is one of Dr. Karp's 5 Ss for helping a baby adjust to life outside the womb. We can mimic the movement they're used to by using swinging, bouncing, and rocking to help calm them.

- **Swinging and Rocking** - Mimics the side to side or front to back movement that babies experience during pregnancy.
- **Bouncing** - Much like swinging, bouncing mimics the movements the baby experiences in utero. The type of bouncing used is more of a jiggling, fast but small movement, of the baby's body while supporting the neck and head.

Supporting the Client:

D	Ask, "What would you like me to do to help you today?"
I	Ask excitedly, "Want to give the baby a bath and shampoo her hair today?"
S	"What can we do today to help you feel even more confident?"
C	"Why don't you keep a list of your questions or concerns from the day before and we can address them when I arrive each day?"

D	I	S	C
Dominant	Inspirational	Supportive	Cautious
Driven	Influential	Submissive	Competent
Demanding	Induces emotion	Stable	Calculating
Determined	Impressive	Security minded	Concerned
Decisive	Interactive	Sentimental	Compliant
Delegates	Interested in people	Safe	Contemplative

Notes:

Overstimulation

It is not uncommon for newborns to get overstimulated. This is a bright and loud new world they have entered and developmentally they do not have the skills to shut out all the stimulants - the smells, the sounds, the lights - surrounding them. And when new babies do become overstimulated, the usual soothing techniques may not be enough to comfort them.

So what can we do for an overstimulated baby?

- Relax. You can remind your client that the baby used to live INSIDE of them and thus responds appropriately to their stress/peace levels.
- Let the client know it is okay to take a minute to regroup. Make sure the baby is safe, step away, and then start again.
- Take the baby to the quietest, darkest room in the house (such as a walk-in closet). The goal is to reduce stimuli as quickly as possible. Walking, jiggling, position changes, and passing the baby off to another person INCREASES stimulation.
- Wrap the baby snugly in a blanket, which has been washed in whatever scents the baby is accustomed to.
- Pull the baby in close to the chest, while holding firmly. Pat the baby's bottom consistently, while making a strong "SHHHH" sound.
- Stay the course. Resist the temptation to soothe the baby's crying by standing, walking, singing, etc.

Sitting on a birth ball while doing this will be more comfortable and will allow the client to maintain this position long enough for the baby to seek comfort from this.

Remember ALL 5 of the baby's senses: sight, smell, taste, touch, and sound. As each becomes increasingly more stimulated, the baby will become more overwhelmed. Learn to recognize what triggers overstimulation for the baby and intervene by decreasing stimulation before it's too late.

Sleep Shaping

Sleep shaping for babies is based on the idea that when very consistent routines are in place around feeding times, wake times, and sleep times, babies will naturally begin to sleep longer and more consistently. This applies exclusively to babies who are healthy and thriving.

Daytime Consistency is Key

- Nutritive feeds are essential
- Feeding the baby on the schedule, regardless of sleep
- Waking the baby to feed if necessary
- Location is the same during each feeding
- Day feeds happen in the same chair, same room, same place with consistent lighting
- The baby is fed and becomes sleepy
- When the baby becomes sleepy, the baby is burped, changed, and the feeding is continued
- After the feed is finished, the baby is awake and interactive for a short period of time, then will demonstrate cues that indicate the baby is ready for sleep

Sleep Readiness Cues

- Gazing off
- Fussiness
- Redness around the eyes
- Yawning

The "Big Sleep"

- Create a "big sleep" routine
- The key to the routine of nighttime sleep is that it is different from daytime sleep, but still consistent
- Bathe the baby
- Change the baby's clothing
- Create a dimly lit, peaceful, sleep space
- Choose a book or song and consistently read or sing that same one each night as part of the "big sleep" preparation routine
- Do not wake the baby for feedings during the night
- When the baby does wake to eat, feed them with limited interaction
- This enables the baby to stay drowsy and sleepy

Family evening routine example:

- The baby eats at 8:00pm, the next feeding is scheduled for 10:30pm.
- Before the baby is woken for the 10:30pm feed, parents can pre-

pare for their own sleep. This will enable them to maximize their own sleep once the baby has been fed and is asleep.
- Prepare for the baby's "big sleep" routine before it begins (bath items, change of clothes, swaddle blanket, etc.).
- Wake the baby at 10:15pm.
- Bathe the baby.
- Change the baby into their nighttime clothes.
- Begin the feeding at 10:30pm in the nighttime feeding location.
- After the feed, enjoy some peaceful time with the baby as they settle down and become sleepy (not fully asleep).
- Swaddle the baby.
- Hold and/or pat the baby for comfort and then lay the baby down.

*Crying is an indication to pick the baby back up and hold them for comfort. Once the baby has settled, place the baby down again. Holding or patting the baby while they are in the sleep position is another way to provide comfort without picking them back up. Repeat until the baby is cozy and peaceful.

Baby-Directed Sleep

Baby-directed sleep allows the baby to determine his or her own sleep/wake cycles and the family accommodates the baby's schedule by altering theirs. There are three common reasons for baby-directed sleep:

- Convenience
- Frustration
- Philosophy

For some parents, baby-directed sleep is part of a larger attachment parenting philosophy. For those who choose baby-directed sleep for convenience, molding their world around their baby's needs may be another facet to their parenting style.

Parents who choose baby-directed sleep out of frustration may not be aware of other alternatives.

Notes:

Safe Infant Sleep

For parents aligned with the philosophy of scheduled parenting, getting their baby to sleep is often a high priority.

Our job as Postpartum & Infant Care Doulas is to both offer education and to support the family's choices surrounding sleep. There is a lot of conflicting information surrounding infant sleep available to parents today.

As doulas, we must stay up-to-date on the recommendations from the American Academy of Pediatrics (AAP), and be unbiased in supporting differing parenting styles and the choices our clients may make regarding infant sleep. Yet, as professional doulas we must always adhere to the highest safety standards when it comes to sleeping infants in our care.

SUID/SIDS

Sudden Unexpected Infant Death (SUID) is the umbrella term used to identify infants who have died unexpectedly under the age of 1 year, where the cause of death was not obvious before investigation. According to the Centers for Disease Control (CDC) there are about 3,400 SUID deaths each year in the United States

The CDC, in an attempt to clarify the issue, suggested that SUID be used as a broad term that encompasses all sudden infant deaths. This would include SIDS, accidental deaths, such as suffocation and strangulation, sudden natural deaths, such as those caused from infections, cardiac, metabolic disorders or neurological conditions, and homicides.

According to the CDC there are three commonly reported categories of SUID:

- Sudden infant death syndrome (SIDS)
- Unknown cause
- Accidental suffocation and strangulation in bed
  "In 2020, there were about 1,389 deaths due to SIDS, about 1,062 deaths due to unknown causes, and about 905 deaths due to accidental suffocation and strangulation in bed."

SUID cases were reported as shown below:

- Sudden infant death syndrome (41%)

- Unknown cause (32%)
- Accidental suffocation and strangulation in bed (27%)

In June of 2023 a study published in the Journal of Neuropathology & Experimental Neurology, discovered that a faulty chemical receptor in the brainstem contributed to SIDS. The serotonin 2A/C receptor is believed to play a vital role in prompting a sleeping baby to wake up and gasp for air when their oxygen levels fall. It is important to remember that this discovery is just one part of the overall puzzle of what contributes to SIDS. SIDS results from a complex combination of biological and environmental factors.

Source: Altered 5-HT2A/C receptor binding in the medulla oblongata in the sudden infant death syndrome (SIDS): Part I. Journal of Neuropathology & Experimental Neurology, Volume 82, Issue 6

While there is no way to effectively prevent SUID or SIDS entirely, the Back to Sleep campaign, now known as the Safe to Sleep campaign, has made strides to help educate families on safe sleep practices in order to eliminate unnecessary risk to babies under the age of 1.

Safe to Sleep Guidelines	
• Infants should be placed on their backs to sleep	• Infants should sleep in a safety-approved crib, play yard, or bassinet
• Car seats and other sitting devices are not recommended for routine sleep at home or in the hospital, especially for young infants	• Room-sharing without bed-sharing is recommended
• Pillows, quilts, comforters, sheepskins, and other soft surfaces are hazardous when placed under the infant or loose in the sleep environment	• Pregnant women should seek and obtain regular prenatal care
• Smoking during pregnancy and in the infant's environment should be avoided	• Avoid illicit drug use during pregnancy and after the infant's birth

• If a breastfeeding mother brings the infant to the adult bed for nursing, the infant should be returned to a separate sleep surface when the mother is ready for sleep	• Consider offering a pacifier at nap and bedtime • Avoid overheating and covering the infant's head

Source: The American Academy of Pediatrics

As a ProDoula Postpartum & Infant Care Doula, you are required to follow the AAP's Safe to Sleep Guidelines when you are the adult in charge of a sleeping infant. Most importantly, this means that when a sleeping baby is in your care you will:

- Place the baby to sleep on their back
- Only use a flat, safe sleeping surface for the baby
- Remove any suffocation or choking hazards from the sleep space
- Make sure the baby is sleeping alone, with no other person, in that safe sleep space

Infant sleep positioning is a complex topic. While families may understand that back sleeping is the safest position for their baby to sleep in, many may find that tummy/side sleep or upright/inclined sleep may improve the quality and quantity of sleep for their baby. When new parents are suffering from exhaustion and sleep deprivation, they may make decisions regarding infant sleep out of desperation rather than deliberation. As Postpartum & Infant Care Doulas, it's our job to provide education on safe sleep in a manner that is compassionate, understanding, and judgment free.

Many new parents may not know the risks of unsafe sleep positions. Inclined sleeping can increase the risk of positional asphyxiation if the baby's chin falls to their chest and closes off their airways. However, for babies with reflux or that deal with a large amount of spit up, parents may be tempted to incline the baby's sleep space. They may even receive outdated advice from a pediatrician to do this. But a sleep space with an incline of more than ten degrees is unsafe and can increase the risk of positional asphyxiation.

Sleep-Related Infant Deaths: Updated 2022 Recommendations for Reducing Infant Deaths in the Sleep Environment, AAP Publications, 2022.

Side and tummy sleeping may also be appealing to sleep-deprived parents if they notice their babies sleep longer stretches in these positions. However, from birth to 8 weeks it is physically more difficult for the baby's body to manage their cardiovascular system, which can lead to decreased oxygen to the brain when sleeping in these positions. Tummy and side sleeping can also increase the risk of rebreathing exhaled air, which may result in decreased oxygen and increased carbon dioxide.

As new families define their parenting philosophies, scheduled parenting and attachment parenting will play a role when it comes to the choices families may make about their baby's sleep. Some families may gravitate towards baby-led sleep while others will feel more aligned with sleep-shaping. Your clients get to choose what is best for them. Your role is to provide non-judgmental, evidence-based information for those families needing guidance. And to always adhere to the highest safety standards for our industry when you are the adult in charge of infant sleep.

Notes:

Infant Feeding

Infant feeding covers the range of ways that a family may choose to feed their baby - breast or chest feeding, pumping and bottle feeding, or formula feeding. Or a combination of any of those methods. Infant feeding can be a complex topic that can come with many complicated emotions for your client. Be prepared to provide evidence-based information on any of these feeding modalities as well as emotional support for the client that is struggling with their feeding journey.

As doulas, we respect that the decision of how one chooses to feed their baby is a deeply personal one, and we support the feeding method chosen by our clients without judgment.

This is a vast topic. If you find yourself wanting to know more, consider taking ProDoula's Infant Feeding Educator Certification to not only expand your knowledge in this field but equip you to offer exceptional Infant Feeding Education as a part of your business model.

Breast/Chest Feeding

Bodyfeeding is an expansive subject. In this section we will only discuss the most basic tenets.

The benefits of breast or chest feeding extend well beyond basic nutrition. In addition to containing all of the vitamins and nutrients the baby needs in the first six months of life, breast milk is packed with disease fighting antibodies that protect the baby from illness.

In the United States, the American Academy of Pediatrics (AAP) currently recommends:

- Infants should be fed breast milk exclusively for the first 6 months after birth. Exclusive breastfeeding means that the infant does not receive any additional foods (except vitamin D) or fluids unless medically recommended.
- After the first 6 months continued breastfeeding with complementary foods for at least 2 years and beyond as mutually desired

Source: American Academy of Pediatrics. (2012). Breastfeeding and the use of human milk. Pediatrics, 129(3), e827–e841

The American Academy of Pediatrics recognizes the following benefits of breastfeeding for the infant:

- Protects against late-onset sepsis in premature infants
- Protects the baby from diarrhea, urinary tract infections, respiratory tract infections, ear infections, and necrotizing enterocolitis
- Reduces the risk of type 1 and type 2 diabetes
- Protects against lymphoma, leukemia, and Hodgkin's disease
- Lowers the baby's risk of SIDS by up to 60%
- Offers the baby ideal nutrition (adjusting as the baby grows)
- Provides for physical closeness
- Reduces the risk of obesity

The following benefits are also recognized by the American Academy of Pediatrics for the birthing parent:

- Reduces postpartum bleeding
- Releases the hormone oxytocin, which helps the uterus return to its pre-pregnancy size
- Burns approximately 300-500 calories a day and may help aid in postpartum weight-loss
- Lowers risk of breast and ovarian cancers
- Reduces stress levels and decreases the risk of postpartum mood disorders

Establishing Breast or Chest Feeding

The Asymmetric Latch

The asymmetric latch allows for a deeper and arguably more effective latch. The asymmetric latch results in the baby's chin touching the breast or chest and their nose being free of the tissue. With this latch, the baby will cover more of the areola with the lower lip, as compared to the upper lip.

To achieve an asymmetric latch, wait for the baby to open their mouth wide. Bring the baby to the body so their chin touches the breast or chest and the head is tilted slightly back. This will result in the chin being pressed into the tissue and the nose being free from the breast once the baby is latched. For some, in the early days this approach may be best facilitated by using the football hold.

With the asymmetric latch the nipple and areola are drawn more deeply into the baby's mouth enabling more contact with the baby's lower jaw, gums, and tongue.

This increased contact with the structures of the lower jaw and mouth in the infant serves to more effectively stimulate the body to increase flow and enhance the release of milk during the feed. This latch technique can also be more beneficial to babies who may have lip or tongue-ties.

Bodyfeeding Positions

The best position is one where both client and baby are comfortable and relaxed. The client should not have to strain to hold the position to keep nursing. These are some common positions for breast or chest feeding that you can present to the client:

> **Cross Cradle Position.** To feed on the left side, the client will support the baby's head with their right hand and fingers while supporting the baby with their right forearm. The client will bring the baby belly-to-belly and nose-to-nipple with the body. The client may use the left hand to manipulate the breast if necessary.
>
> **Football Position.** Lay the baby's back along the client's forearm so that they are holding the baby like a football while supporting his or her head and neck with their palm. This works best with newborns and small babies. It's also a good position if the client is recovering from a cesarean birth and needs to protect their belly from the pressure or weight of the baby.
>
> **Side-Lying Position.** This position is great for night feedings in bed. Side-lying also works well if the client is recovering from an episiotomy (an incision to widen the vaginal opening during delivery). First, use pillows under the client's head to help them get comfortable. Then have the client snuggle close to the baby and use their free hand to lift the breast and nipple into the baby's mouth. Once the baby is correctly "latched on," the client will support the baby's head and neck with their free hand so there is no twisting or straining to continue nursing.

Determining Adequate Intake

Tracking Diapers

One of the best ways to determine that an exclusively breast or chest fed baby is getting enough to eat is to track the number of wet and soiled diapers they produce in a 24-hour period.

- By day 4 postpartum, the infant should produce 6-8 wet and 1-3 soiled diapers per day. (Between days 1-3 of life, the overall output is less. Expect 1-3 wet and soiled diapers each.)

Parents may wish to track these numbers by whatever means is most convenient for them - a tracking app or just pen and paper. An infant that is getting enough milk at the body will have skin that appears well hydrated and will seem satiated after a feed. They will have periods of contentment around feedings.

Frequent Feeding

The exclusively breast or chest fed newborn will eat at the body anywhere from 8-12 times in a 24-hour period and on average every 2-3 hours. The time between feeds is measured from the start of one feeding session to the start of the next. If the baby is sleeping for too long throughout the day and/or not waking to eat on their own, the parents will likely be advised to wake the baby and initiate the feeding session.

Active Feeding

The newborn should feed actively, with a continuous pattern of vigorous nutritive sucks and swallows, followed by brief pauses. A baby that is pausing for too long or sleeping at the breast or chest too frequently may not effectively transfer milk during a feeding. Breast compression and massage, whereby the bodyfeeding parent firmly squeezes down and toward the nipple across many parts of the breast, can encourage milk to flow into the baby's mouth and reignite interest in the feed.

A baby that is struggling to get enough milk at the breast or chest may:

- Appear lethargic or sleep too often without waking to eat
- Have inadequate wet and dirty diapers
- Fall asleep easily at the body and have difficulty being roused to

eat
- Show signs of dehydration such as a sunken fontanelle, dry skin, and chapped lips

24 Hour Feeding and Diapering Chart Example

Name:		Date:		
Time	Breast	Bottle	Wet Diaper	Dirty Diaper
am / pm	min. L R	oz.		
am / pm	min L R	oz.		
am / pm	min L R	oz.		
am / pm	min L R	oz.		
am / pm	min L R	oz.		
am / pm	min L R	oz.		
am / pm	min L R	oz.		
am / pm	min L R	oz.		

Challenges with Breast or Chest Feeding

Sore Nipples – In early bodyfeeding it is normal for the lactating parent to expect some nipple soreness. Their nipples have never been utilized in this capacity! Assist the client in proper latch and teach them to use their finger to break the suction when taking the baby off the breast.

Dry, Cracked Nipples – Encourage clients to eliminate perfumes, soaps, creams, or body products that contain alcohol as they can cause dryness. The best solution for dry nipples is to hand express some milk and spread it over the nipple and let it air dry. Bleeding nipples heal faster using the protocol for "wet wound healing." Keep the nipples moist with products such as nipple ointments and gel pads. Clients may wish to contact their healthcare provider for a prescription for All Purpose Nipple Ointment to promote even faster healing.

Worries About Milk Production – A baby who is getting an adequate milk supply should be wetting six to eight diapers a day. The size or shape of a client's breast has no bearing on milk production. Consistent breastfeeding is a stimulant for building supply. A client with milk supply issues should seek advice from an IBCLC (International Board Certified Lactation Consultant).

Flat or Inverted Nipples – In cases such as these, the nipple is either flat or retracted into the breast. A doula or IBCLC can encourage this lactating parent to try manual stimulation of the nipple or use a pump to pull the nipple forward. Another option is to use a nipple shield at the recommendation of an IBCLC. If the flat nipples are caused by engorgement, rather than anatomy, the client can also use reverse pressure softening to soften and draw out the nipple before latching the baby.

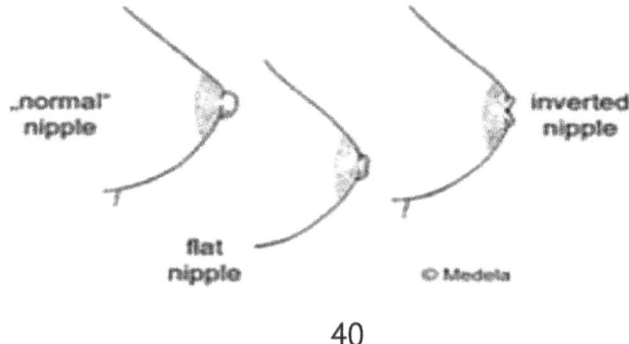

40

Engorgement – Breast fullness is common in bodyfeeding parents. It happens most often during the first week postpartum as the milk transitions from colostrum to mature milk. Engorgement occurs when the milk ducts in the breast or chest have become congested. Fluid is trapped in the breasts and it makes them feel hard, painful, and swollen. Applying cold packs can relieve mild symptoms (heat should be avoided as it can exacerbate inflammation). Expressing milk, either by releasing milk by hand or pump, can also help but will encourage more production if done too frequently.

Inflammation/Infection (Mastitis) – Historically mastitis has been viewed as a singular pathology of the lactating breast or chest. However, new evidence demonstrates that mastitis lies on a spectrum of conditions resulting from inflammation of the supportive tissues as well as inflammation of the ductal structures. While mastitis is used as a general term, there are a variety of subsets of mastitis that exist. As a result of the new evidence, the Academy of Breastfeeding Medicine has updated its protocol surrounding how best to approach mastitis.

Ductal narrowing, inflammatory mastitis, bacterial mastitis, and breast abscess now all fall under the main category of mastitis as an inflammatory condition. Symptoms of mastitis include pain, swelling, and warmth of the breast or chest; red streaking extending out from the area of infection can be present. The individual may have a fever of 101.3° F or higher, along with flu-like symptoms such as body aches and chills.

Due to this challenge now being recognized as a problem with inflammation, the Academy of Breastfeeding Medicine no longer recommends using heat to deal with any subset of mastitis as heat can further inflame the tissue.

Ductal Inflammation/Blocked Ducts – A single sore spot on the breast or chest, which may also appear red and hot to the touch, can signal inflammation in the ductal tissue, which can slow or hinder the easy flow of milk through the ducts. This phenomenon is now recognized along the early spectrum of mastitis. According to the new Academy of Breastfeeding Medicine Protocols, using a cold pack along with over the counter anti-inflammatories can relieve the inflammation and reduce the ductal narrowing. Heat should be avoided. More frequent nursing is also beneficial.

Stress – Being overly anxious or stressed can interfere with the letdown reflex. That's the body's natural release of milk into the milk ducts. The letdown reflex is triggered by the hormone oxytocin and is released when the baby nurses. The let-down reflex can also be triggered just by the lactating person hearing their baby cry or thinking about their baby. Helping the client stay as relaxed and calm as possible before and during feeding sessions can help milk let down and flow more easily.

Thrush – A form of yeast. If suspected, encourage the client to see their physician, midwife, or IBCLC for diagnosis. Symptoms may include pink or red discoloration on or around the nipples and sharp pain (almost like shards of glass) into the breast or chest for the client. Symptoms for the baby include white patches on the tongue, cheeks, and gums.

B.A.S.I.C.S. of Bodyfeeding - share with your clients:

- **B**e patient
- **A**ffirmations
- **S**oothe your body
- **I**nformation
- **C**omfort
- **S**erenity

Breast or Chest Feeding Red Flags - The Baby

Inadequate Weight Gain

It is considered normal for the average newborn to lose weight after birth. It is expected that a healthy newborn may lose approximately 7-10% of their birth weight after birth, and regain that weight within the first few weeks post birth.

During the first month of life most newborns gain about 1 ounce per day and grow in length by about 1 to 1 1/2 inches. Common periods of rapid growth, or "growth spurts," tend to occur around day 7-10 and at 3 weeks and 6 weeks of age.

Inadequate Feeding Pattern

While the exact quantity of milk cannot be precisely measured, it is expected that the average breast or chest fed newborn will feed 8 or more times in a 24-hour period, or approximately every 2-3 hours. Formula fed babies tend to eat less often and the average interval between feeds tends to be every 3-4 hours.

During a growth spurt, the bodyfed baby may cluster feed or have many feeds in a row that come much more closely together. At times, they may seem to be unsatisfied at the breast or chest, popping off the nipple and latching back on.

Tongue and Lip Ties

Every person has some degree of tissue (frenum) under the tongue and at the upper lip where the lip joins the gums. When this tissue restricts the movement or mobility of the tongue it is considered a 'tie'. Some babies will be able to bodyfeed without issue, and for others the tie may make breast or chest feeding, bottle-feeding and even pacifier sucking difficult. Tongue-ties can make it difficult for babies to obtain and maintain a secure latch on the breast or chest. Often, babies will try to compensate for this by sucking harder which can contribute to nipple damage and pain. When a baby who is tongue-tied can no longer maintain a secure latch, the suction breaks temporarily and a clicking sound may be heard.

Clicking at the breast or chest throughout the feed can be an indicator of tongue-tie.

Tongue-ties can also prevent the baby from drawing the nipple deeply into the mouth and placing it behind the hard palate and onto the soft palate where it is protected from pinching and abrasion.

Other indicators of possible tongue-tie that may be seen in the infant include:

- Poor latch
- Clicking while feeding
- Repeated breaking of suction while at the breast or chest
- Slow weight gain
- Infrequent swallowing
- Fussiness and/or arching at the breast or chest
- Breast tissue slips in and out of baby's mouth while feeding
- Leaking milk out of mouth during a feed
- Tiring at the breast/chest within a few minutes of beginning the feed
- Symptoms of colic or reflux

Alternative Means of Milk Transfer

Breast or chest feeding may offer challenges in the early days and weeks after birth. In this section, we will introduce some alternative options to feeding a baby other than directly from the body.

The following descriptions are included only to help familiarize and prepare you to support a client who is taking advantage of one of these recommendations. As a doula, you will NOT be the one recommending these alternative means of milk transfer to your clients.

As a Postpartum & Infant Care Doula, your primary role is to recognize the signs of successful bodyfeeding and the signs and symptoms which may indicate that additional help may be needed.

An exclusively breast or chest feeding baby who is feeding well:

- Has adequate wet and soiled diapers - 6-8 wet diapers and 1-3 soiled diapers per 24 hours by day 4 post birth
  - Prior to day 4, wet diapers will equal the number of days old for the baby
- Feeds actively from the body
- Has skin that appears well-hydrated
- Has periods of wakefulness

A baby who is struggling with feeding may:

- Appear lethargic
- Have inadequate wet and soiled diapers
- May fall asleep easily at the breast or chest
- May appear dehydrated; signs of dehydration may include:
  - Dry skin
  - Chapped lips
  - Sunken fontanelle

Should the doula notice that the baby is showing signs of dehydration, a referral back to the baby's pediatrician or the client's IBCLC should be made IMMEDIATELY for further evaluation and possible intervention.

If the doula observes signs or symptoms that may be concerning, it is appropriate to bring these concerns to the client's attention.

- "I'm seeing a few signs that the baby may not be feeding as well as we'd like at the breast. Based on these signs, I feel it is important for you to consult with your baby's pediatrician or a lactation professional."
    - It is important that the doula has identified a qualified lactation professional in their community to refer clients to.
- While underlying issues are being identified and resolved, Rule #1 of infant feeding is, "Feed the baby."
    - This can be achieved by providing the baby with pumped milk, donor milk, or formula.
    - You can ask the client, "Which option feels best for us to explore at this time?"

If the client desires to continue bodyfeeding after resolving the underlying feeding issues, an IBCLC or pediatrician may advise Triple Feeding, a regimen that involves bringing the baby to the body to feed for a certain amount of time, followed by expressing milk with a pump, and then feeding the baby the supplemental milk using one of the tools below.

The client may choose to use one of the tools below to supplement their baby with donor milk or formula if they prefer not to use a pump. Triple Feeding is a temporary solution and not a sustainable, long-term feeding method.

Nipple Shield – A soft, flexible covering for the nipple that is used over the client's nipple to assist with the baby's latch.

- To apply the nipple shield, the client flips the nipple shield's edges up and applies the center of the shield to the center of the nipple. The client will then smooth the edges down flat against the breast. If the shield isn't staying adhered to the breast or chest, the edges of the shield can be moistened before application.

Cup Feeding – A small, soft silicone cup that is used with small amounts of milk or formula to feed the baby.

- The cup is held against the baby's bottom lip and the baby is given the opportunity to smell the milk. With the cup tipped so that the milk just touches the baby's bottom lip, the baby will begin sticking his or her tongue out and begin to "taste" the milk and lap it up like a kitten. It is important that care is taken to not pour milk into the baby's mouth, as this may cause choking or aspiration of the milk into the baby's lungs.

Finger Feeding - A #5 French feeding tube and a container or syringe to hold formula or milk is used to transfer food to the baby.

- The tube is placed into a bottle of milk or formula or attached to a syringe. The tube is fed along the caregiver's finger and the baby is allowed to suck on the caregiver's finger while the food is delivered through the tube. If a syringe is used, it is important to not squirt the milk or formula through the tube and into the baby's mouth. A slow, steady depression of the syringe is necessary to ensure that the baby does not choke or aspirate the milk into their lungs.

Bottle Feeding - When supplementation with a bottle is necessary, it is common for clients to worry about nipple confusion. An alternative consideration may be that the baby has a flow preference. When introducing bottle feeds to a breast or chest fed baby, it is important to use the slowest flow nipple and offer education to the parents regarding paced feeding. (Paced Bottle Feeding will be discussed in more detail on page 130.)

Expression and Storage of Milk

This section will cover the equipment and devices, along with proper storage and warming guidelines, for expressed milk.

Breast Pumps

There are two basic types of pumps available on the market (although there are many different models sold by various companies).

- Manual pumps
- Electric pumps

Manual Pumps

Designed for occasional use, manual, hand-held pumps are typically used for emergency situations, such as when the lactating parent and the baby will be separated for a short period of time or when occasional pumping is necessary.

Electric Breast Pumps

There are three kinds of electric pumps.

- Battery or electric operated pumps for occasional use.
- Full electric pumps that can be used throughout the client's nursing relationship on a regular basis.
    - These electric pumps are intended for use by a single user.
- Hospital grade electric pumps that are intended for frequent pumping and are best suited for the client whose baby is less than 8 weeks old and whose milk supply has not yet been established.
    - Hospital grade pumps are often rented and can be used by more than one user.

Instructions for pumps will vary by model, design, and manufacturer. We encourage you to become familiar with a variety of pumps.

Breast Pump Flanges

When choosing to express milk via a pump, it is important that the proper size flange be used. The full electric pumps typically come with a standard sized flange, but many sizes are available from the manufacturer.

When determining proper fit:

- If the nipple rubs against the inside of the flange while the client is pumping, the flange may be too small.
- If the areola is also pulled down into the flange as the client is pumping, the flange size may be too large.
- If the client is having difficulty with pumping, they may need to see a qualified lactation professional to make sure they are using properly sized flanges.

Manual Expression

Manual or hand expression of milk is a useful skill for any nursing individual. Some clients may choose to not make pumping a part of their bodyfeeding relationship and instead use hand expression to help maintain comfort when away from their baby. Others may find they do not respond well to manual or electric pumps and can express more milk by hand. If a lactating individual is away from their baby for an unexpected amount of time, using hand expression can help bring comfort by relieving engorgement.

While there are many approaches to hand expression, there are a few basic tips to be aware of:

- The client may wish to massage the breasts or place a warm towel over the chest before beginning to help milk flow more readily.
- The client may find that sitting upright and leaning slightly forward also encourages milk flow.
- The client will cup the breast with the thumb on top and the fingers beneath the breast. With the thumb and forefinger just behind the outer edge of the areola, they will then press in towards their chest wall while gently compressing the breast.
- They will continue pressing into the chest wall while compressing the breast and bringing the thumb and index finger together just behind the areola by pressing into the breast, not pulling out on the areola/nipple.

- The client may need to adjust their grip to find the best spot/angle to allow the milk to begin to flow.
- Once the milk begins to flow, the client may use a rhythmic cycle of compress, press, and relaxing to simulate the rhythm of a nursing baby.
- The client should rotate their hand around the breast to ensure that they are compressing all areas of the chest during expression.
- Repeat on the opposite side.

Milk Storage and Warming

When storing expressed milk, there are three basic options:

- Storage in bottles
- Storage in bags
- Storage in pouches

Storage in Bottles – Clients will indicate their preference for glass or plastic bottles. Both glass and plastic bottles can be washed and reused and are more durable than plastic milk storage bags or pouches.

Storage in Bags or Pouches – Some clients may prefer the space saving option of storing their milk in plastic pumping bags or pouches. Plastic bags are designed for specific pumping systems and often connect directly to the bottom of the pumping flange so that milk may be collected directly into the bag. Other clients may prefer to pump directly into a bottle and then transfer the milk into the bags for storage.

The following guidelines are for storing milk for healthy term infants.

Expressed Milk Guidelines: Freshly Expressed Milk			
Room Temperature	Cooler with Frozen Ice Pack	Refrigerator	Freezer
Up to 4 hours at 77° F or less	24 hours at 59° F or less	4 days at 39° F or lower	6-12 months at 0-4° F

Reference: Office Of Women's Health

Please note that storage guidelines will often vary slightly depending on the source.

In order to prevent wasting milk that is not consumed during a feed, it is recommended that expressed milk be stored in 1-4 ounce portions. Clients can label their milk with the date it was pumped. Milk that is first stored is first used.

Warming Stored Milk

When milk has been frozen for storage, it must be defrosted before it is warmed. Thawing can be achieved by overnight refrigeration. If quicker thawing is needed, running the bottle or storage bag under cool running water and increasing the temperature of the water slowly can be effective. Milk that has been previously frozen can be stored in the refrigerator for up to 24 hours, but should NOT be refrozen.

Breastmilk that has been defrosted or stored in a refrigerator or cooler may separate. The cream will rise to the top of the milk during storage. To combine the milk, it is perfectly acceptable to shake or swirl the separated milk back together. There is no scientific evidence to support the rule against shaking milk.

To warm milk that has been stored in the refrigerator or a cooler there are two basic options:

- Use a bottle warmer.
- Place the bottle or storage bag in a container filled with warm water.

When using a bottle warmer, make sure to follow the manufacturer's instructions.

When warming in a small container, never use boiling or overly hot water and remember to test the temperature of the bottle before offering it to the baby. To test the temperature of the milk, drip the milk onto the inside of your wrist. The milk should feel warm, but not hot or cold.

Never heat milk or food for an infant in the microwave.

Partial bottles of warmed milk left after a feed may be safe to refrigerate, but must be used within 1-2 hours or be discarded.

Notes:

Bottle Feeding

Cleaning & Sanitizing Bottles

Bottles should be sterilized before their first use, after being purchased, after extended periods of not being used, or if the baby was recently ill.

Methods of Sterilization

- Stove-top with boiling water
- Commercial bottle sanitizer
- Dishwasher on the sterilization setting

Stove-top Sterilization:

1. Pour enough water into a pot so that bottles and nipples will be completely submerged while boiling.
2. Open bottles and separate parts.
3. While water is heating to a boil, wash preliminary grime or bacteria with hot, soapy water.
4. Submerge bottles and all bottle parts into the boiling water.
   a. Allow to soak for 5-10 minutes.
5. Use metal tongs to remove bottles and parts from the pot and place them to dry on a drying rack.

Bottles should be washed in hot, soapy water prior to each subsequent use.

Bottle Nipples

Nipple Shape: Traditional nipples are shaped like a bell or dome. Orthodontic nipples are designed to accommodate the baby's palate and gums and have a bulb that's flat on the side which rests on the baby's tongue. For a baby that will eat from both the breast/chest and the bottle, many IBCLCs recommend a nipple that is more narrow and tapered at the end, as a wide-necked bottle with a wide nipple can result in a more shallow latch from the baby. The design of these wide nipples can make it harder for the baby to take more of the nipple into their mouth, resulting in a latch at the tip of the nipple.

Size and Flow: Nipples come in a range of sizes and a variety of flow rates, from slow to fast. Preemies and newborns usually benefit from the smallest size (often called "stage 1"), which has the slowest flow. Babies graduate to larger sizes with a faster flow as they get older and can suck and swallow more effectively.

Nipples are marked with the size and a suggested age range. Parents may have to try a few different nipple sizes to find one that works best for their baby.

Disposables: Disposable nipples can come in handy when on the go. These are sold prepackaged and sterilized for convenience and are easily placed on a bottle. They are single use and should be discarded after the feeding.

Types of Bottles

Plastic: Plastic baby bottles have plastic bodies, caps, covers, and internal components. These bottles typically have silicone nipples and sometimes silicone valves inside. Most are designed in a basic bottle shape and others are contoured to help make gripping easier. Plastic is considered lighter and often easier to hold. It can be more difficult to clean and more easily scratched, which can lead to bacterial growth and allow odors to develop.

Glass: Glass bottles have a glass body, usually shock resistant borosilicate glass, and a plastic collar with silicone nipple. Some of these bottles offer a silicone sleeve that can help make the bottle easier to hold and offers some protection from occasional dropping. The important thing to note is that glass bottles can and do break so extra care is required. Glass bottles are usually heavier than plastic and the silicone sleeve can make them easier for little ones to hold by themselves. Glass contains no harmful chemicals. They can be sanitized at higher temperatures versus plastic bottles, which eliminates more bacteria. Glass is harder to scratch and contents do not cling to the side to leave behind odors.

Disposables: Bottles with drop-in plastic inserts filled with formula or milk can be handy while on the go and are easy to clean. When the bottle is finished, just toss the liner and wash the nipple. Each insert is intended for single use.

Bottle Shape: Bottles come in a wide variety of shapes. Many on the market claim to be easier for babies to hold and have an ergonomic design. Wide-necked bottles may make measuring formula easier; however, they may not fit into drink-holders on strollers or in cars.

Venting Systems: Many bottles are marketed suggesting they prevent colic. Venting systems or straw-like components are intended to prevent the baby from ingesting air. Venting systems built into the nipple or the bottom of the bottle allow air to escape.

Making Bottle Feeding a Bonding Experience

Feeding a baby can be a bonding experience. Feeling loved and nourished leads to strong bonds. Regardless of feeding choice - body or bottle - skin-to-skin and full engagement during the feed can heighten the experience for both parent and child.

Paced Bottle Feeding

Paced feeding is intended to allow the baby to set the pace for their feedings. For the breast or chest fed baby, it mimics being at the body and may reduce the chance of the baby developing a flow preference. For both bottle-fed and breast or chest fed babies, paced feeding may also reduce the symptoms and discomfort associated with reflux.

How to Pace Feed:

> 1. Hold the baby in a slightly reclined position with their head in line with their back (so that their head is not turned and their chin is not resting on their chest).
> 2. Use a slow flow nipple.
> 3. Allow the baby to draw the nipple into their mouth as opposed to pushing the
> nipple in. This will allow the baby to determine when the feed begins. Stroke the baby's lips from top to bottom with the nipple to elicit a rooting response of a widely opened mouth and allow the baby to "accept" the nipple.
> 4. Keep the bottle horizontal, vertical enough only to keep milk in the nipple.
> 5. Let the baby get 3-4 sucks of milk.
> 6. Gently lower the bottle to slow or stop the flow of milk if the baby is trying to drink
> too fast. It is important to not totally remove the bottle as this may cause stress for the baby. Pausing offers the baby a chance to swallow and control the flow of milk, as well as discourages the baby from guzzling during a feed. Paced feeding mimics the way milk is taken from the body.

7. Raise the bottle to a horizontal position once more to allow a small amount of milk back into the nipple. Allow the baby to have 2-3 sucks and then pause. Repeat throughout the remainder of the feeding.

8. Allow the baby to decide when the feed ends. The baby may indicate they are no longer interested by turning their head away or not pulling the nipple back in after a pause.

A flow of milk that is too strong can make the baby appear as if they are guzzling the milk due to hunger, but they may be just trying to keep up with the flow of milk. Their eyes may widen, their brows may furrow.

Babies who are consistently paced fed will likely begin to pace themselves over time.

Approximate amount a baby takes during feeding:

- Day one: 5-7ml/.50 Tbsp
- Day three: 22-27ml/.75-1oz
- One week: 45-60ml/1.5-2oz
- One month: 80-150ml/2.5-5oz

Burping a Baby

During a feeding, air can get into a baby's stomach causing discomfort and fussiness. Burping helps the baby to release this air. Some pediatricians believe burping may also help reduce spit up and other symptoms of reflux. Most babies outgrow the need to be burped around 4 to 6 months of age.

When to Burp a Baby

When bodyfeeding, it is common to burp the baby when switching from one side to the other. Burping a breast or chest fed baby who is sleeping at the body can wake them and allow them to continue the feed.

A baby who is uncomfortable from excess air during a feed may make facial expressions or seem irritable, which may indicate that burping may be helpful.

How to Burp a Baby

There are several methods to burp a baby.

- On the Chest/Shoulder
    - Place burp cloth over the shoulder.
    - Hold the baby upright, with their chin resting on your shoulder and their abdomen pressed into your chest.
    - Holding the baby with one hand, use the other hand to alternate between rubbing up and down on the baby's back and patting.
    - It is sometimes helpful to start patting on the lower back and work your way up.

- Sitting Up
    - Place the baby's bottom on your lap and support the body with one hand. The palm is supporting the baby's chest and the fingers are supporting the baby's jaw and chin. Be careful not to put pressure on the baby's neck.
    - You may want to place a burp cloth over your hand, making sure it stays away from the baby's face.
    - Use your other hand to alternate between rubbing up and down and patting the baby's back. Sometimes it is helpful to start patting on the lower back and work your way up.

- Across the Lap
    - Place a burp cloth over your lap.
    - Place the baby face down on your legs so the baby is lying across your knees horizontally.
    - Support the baby's chin and jaw with one hand. Make sure the baby's head is not lower than the rest of their body.
    - Use the other hand to alternate between rubbing up and down on the baby's back and patting. Sometimes it is helpful to start patting on the lower back and work your way up.

Reflux

Infant reflux occurs when food backs up (refluxes) from a baby's stomach, causing the baby to spit up. Sometimes called gastroesophageal reflux (GER), the condition is rarely serious and becomes less common as a baby gets older. It's unusual for infant reflux to continue after age 18 months. Reflux occurs in healthy infants multiple times a day. As long as the baby is healthy, content, and growing well, the reflux is not usually a cause for concern.

Rarely, infant reflux can be a sign of a medical problem, such as an allergy, a blockage in the digestive system, or gastroesophageal reflux disease (GERD).

Infant reflux usually clears up by itself. In the meantime, the family's doctor might recommend:

- Giving the baby smaller, more frequent feedings
- Taking breaks during the feed to burp the baby
- Holding baby upright for 20 to 30 minutes after feedings
- Eliminating dairy products, beef, or eggs from the client's diet if breast or chest feeding, to test if the baby has an allergy
- Switching the type of formula the baby is fed
- Using a different size nipple on baby bottles; a nipple that is too large or too small can cause the baby to swallow air
- Thickening formula or expressed milk slightly and in gradual increments with rice cereal
- Medication: Reflux medications are not recommended for children with uncomplicated reflux; these medications can prevent absorption of calcium and iron, and may increase the risk of certain intestinal and respiratory infections

A short-term trial of an acid-blocking medication may be recommended by the baby's pediatrician if the baby:

- Has poor weight gain and other treatments have not worked
- Refuses to feed
- Has evidence of an inflamed esophagus
- Has chronic asthma and reflux

It is never our job to try to diagnose reflux. If the parents suspect there is an issue, encourage them to contact their baby's doctor.

Formula Feeding

Formula Quiz

Can I use hot water from the tap to prepare formula?	Yes	No
Can I add more formula to a bottle the baby has already drank from?	Yes	No
Can formula left over in the bottle be saved and given at the next feed?	Yes	No
How long can prepared bottles of formula be kept at room temperature?		

Answer Key:

- *Because hot water can leach minerals and other build-up found in pipes, only cold water from the tap should be used when preparing formula.*
- *Once a baby drinks from a bottle, bacteria from the baby's mouth is introduced into the formula, which can then multiply. For this reason, we cannot add more formula to a bottle the baby has already drank from.*
- *Once a baby drinks from a bottle, bacteria from the baby's mouth is introduced into the formula, which can then multiply. For this reason, we cannot reuse leftover formula for the next feeding.*
- *Because bacteria can flourish as a prepared bottle of formula sits at room temperature, we must use bottles of formula within one hour of preparation.*

For most families there are two reasons they come to formula feeding:

- Formula feeding by choice
- Formula feeding by necessity

As doulas, our role is to support our clients' choices in an unbiased, non-judgmental way, regardless of our personal choices.

Formula feeding is a topic that can be colored with judgment by friends, family, acquaintances, and random strangers in the grocery store. For some clients, self-judgment and feelings of failure or inadequacy can lead to postpartum mood disorders. This client may need additional support.

While some families may choose to formula feed from the beginning, for others it may be an emotional decision.

Formula Feeding Basics

It is important that infant formula be properly prepared. Improper preparation of formula may lead to inadequate nutrition or problems such as constipation or diarrhea.

Ready to Feed – Ready to feed formula requires no preparation. Formula can be poured directly into bottles and be given to the baby with no need to plan ahead. Ready to feed formula may come in a larger container that can be poured into individual bottles or bought in single serving bottles complete with nipples.

Powdered – Powdered formula is the most popular and often is the most economic choice for families. Water and powder are mixed according to the manufacturer's instructions.

Concentrated – Concentrated formula is mixed with equal parts water and formula and is less time consuming to prepare than powdered formula. Preference should always be the choice of the parents.

Preparation

- **Ready to Feed** – Ready to feed formula can be poured directly into the bottles before a feed and given to the baby immediately.
- **Concentrated** – To prepare, run cold water for 30 seconds, clean the top of the container before opening, and shake well. Add desired amount of water to the bottle, add an equal amount of concentrated formula, cap the bottle, and shake well.
- **Powdered** – Always refer to the manufacturer's instructions for how to prepare powdered formula; do not hard pack formula scoop. Once measured, cap and shake well and feed immediately.

Clients often have questions surrounding the type of water to use when making baby formula. According to the CDC, the only consideration when it comes to water is that it must be from a safe drinking source. This could be from the tap, from a filter on the refrigerator, or from a bottle. As long as it is a safe drinking water source, it is acceptable.

How to Prepare and Store Powdered Infant Formula, Centers for Disease Control and Prevention

Because powdered infant formulas are not sterile, the CDC has further recommendations when preparing powdered formula for babies that are under two months of age, were born prematurely, or have a weakened immune system. Babies in these categories can be susceptible to serious illness or even death from Cronobacter, a germ that can be found in powdered infant formulas. In order to reduce the risk of illness from Cronobacter, the CDC recommends boiling water, allowing it to cool for several minutes, and then adding the powdered formula to the water while it is still at least 158 degrees Fahrenheit or 70 degrees Celsius.

Cronobacter Infection and Infants, Centers of Disease Control and Prevention

Types of Formula

Infant formula is not one size fits all. Most hospitals or pediatricians have a warm line for parents to call when questions arise. If a client who hasn't planned to formula feed has now decided to offer formula, encourage the client to speak to their baby's provider for a recommendation for a formula brand.

For example, premature babies should not be fed formula made from powder, and there are special formulas for infants who are allergic to dairy, have reflux, or other health issues. The choice of formula for your client's baby is best made with the advice and support of their medical care provider.

The Ever-Evolving Role of the Postpartum & Infant Care Doula

As a doula, you are a great asset to the clients that you serve. Your vast knowledge of the physical and emotional components of pregnancy, birth, and the postpartum period will benefit your clients tremendously. It is imperative that as doulas we use this knowledge to encourage clients to feel empowered by their own choices. Do not fall prey to leading with your own opinions. Be careful to present information regarding choices/options in a non-biased way. If your client does not know what you personally would choose, you have been successful in the exchange.

Educate yourself in all aspects of pregnancy, birth, and the postpartum period. Regardless of whether or not you plan to become a labor support doula, the labor doula training will be a valuable tool in helping you have a greater understanding of the postpartum client. If you only have your own birth experiences to compare to your client's experience, you may fall short in understanding the emotional and physical aspects of the client's birth story.

As Postpartum & Infant Care Doulas, we have the opportunity to begin supporting our clients as early as their first few days post birth. Our support often continues for weeks, months, and even throughout the first year of the baby's life. Your clients will look to you for guidance at each of these stages and your role is to be able to meet them where they are and prepare them for what is to come.

Understand that your support will change as the baby gets older and the parents become more confident and equipped. The early days and weeks might be focused heavily on feeding support and the emotional adjustment to new parenthood. As the weeks go on, clients will look to you for advice on infant sleep, transitioning back to work, or introducing solids, for example.

Our clients turn to us with such important topics because - if we have given them our non-judgmental support and professionalism - they view us as an extension of their parenting partnership. We become one of the few persons in their life that supports them without bias and helps them navigate big parenting choices without any agenda of our own. This is what makes postpartum doula support so valuable. Provide this for your clients and they will come back to you again and again.

Entry Level Business for Doulas

For most doulas training and working with clients is the focus, and that's great because it should be! However, an equal amount of focus must be placed on becoming a doula business owner. ProDoula is committed to supporting you as you begin this new chapter in your life. In addition to the support you will receive from the ProDoula Training & Development Team and the Home Office, there are numerous resources available to you on the ProDoula website, www. prodoula.com.

In the ProDoula online shop, you can find various digital downloads and services to help get your business running smoothly and successfully.

ProDoula's Doula Learning Channel (www. doulalearningchannel.com) is another great resource that will assist you with short, comprehensive courses that will enrich you personally, practically, and professionally.

Starting a Doula Business - What You Will Need

A Business Name

Before you can complete some of the following tasks, you will need to settle on a name for your business. Remember to take into account the importance of things like branding and search engine optimization (SEO), rather than what personally appeals to you, when deciding on a name for your new business.

ProDoula's Beginner's Business Training or private business consulting with ProDoula's CEO, Randy Patterson, can assist you with creating a brand, including a name and logo, if you need help in this area.

Business Structure

In order to run a professional doula business, you must establish your business under a recognized legal structure for your state. This might be a Limited Liability Company (LLC), an S-Corporation (S-Corp), or even just Doing Business As (DBA). Enlist the help of a professional, such as an attorney or an accountant, to determine which is the right structure for you.

In most states you will need to have a recognized legal business structure before you can apply for an Employer Identification Number (EIN) or open a business bank account, both of which are important for a professional doula business.

What Doula Business Model Is Right For You?

Become An Independent Doula

This will allow you to make your own rules. You will decide how many clients you will serve, how you will market and sell your services, and what those services will be. With the freedom and flexibility to make all of your own rules comes responsibility and pressure, which can be overwhelming or unfamiliar.

ProDoula will help you navigate and overcome these challenges by:

- Offering you strategies, support, and systems that will contribute to your confidence.
- Providing advice on establishing your business and creating the balance that is right for you and your family.
- Making the necessary courses and consultations available to you as you develop and grow your business.

Own A Doula Agency

For the entrepreneur-turned-doula or doula-turned-entrepreneur, this is a rewarding opportunity, both personally and financially.

It puts you in the driver's seat, setting an agency agenda and becoming a leader. In this scenario, you are responsible for your own financial success, but you also contribute to the financial success of the independent contractors that your agency offers work to. It can be stressful and overwhelming but also incredibly rewarding.

ProDoula can provide a tremendous amount of support and advice by:

- Sharing the company history of Northeast Doulas – the successful doula agency established by the founders of ProDoula.
- Providing guidance on how to find, train, and inspire doulas.
- Guiding you on how to set up the relationship – financially as well as the legal structure and business flow of information.
- Providing templates for contracts between your business and clients and subcontractor.
- Providing strategies and resources for various marketing and net-

work strategies necessary to keep your doulas working.
- And so much more!

Work For An Agency

Consider working for a doula agency as an employee or independent contractor. This type of work allows you to work for clients without any of the time or expenses associated with finding those clients. You will be paid for the time you are working, although at a rate that is lower than what you would earn as an independent doula.

ProDoula can provide you guidance to:

- Establish all necessary legal/financial protections for yourself – setting up LLC, insurance, etc.
- Establish boundaries and clear communication with the agency owner.
- Negotiate pay/terms and conditions of contract with the agency.

Decide on Pricing

Setting the fee for your service is one of the most important decisions you will make for your doula business. The prices you begin with can either support your future growth or hold you back.

Do not allow others or your own negative thinking to deter you from charging fair and competitive compensation for your dedication and service to your clients. Your investment of time, money, and personal sacrifice deserves to be compensated.

A largely debated topic is the decision to include or exclude prices on your website. While this is certainly an individual decision, it is important to remember that expectant families are not just buying a doula. They are buying a relationship with a doula. Regardless of how well written your website is, without having a discussion by phone or in-person with you, the individual can not determine whether or not you are worth the price listed. For that reason, ProDoula recommends that you do not list your prices on your website but rather discuss them with the potential client when speaking with them.

Insurance Coverage/Reimbursement

As doula support becomes more mainstream, increasingly companies are offering benefits that cover or reimburse for doula services, such as Carrot Fertility. Some states are even including doula coverage in their Medicaid benefits. These options can allow more people to benefit from doula support, however, it is important to consider what this will require of you as a business owner.

Companies that reimburse for doula services will normally create their own requirements for which doula services are eligible. Almost all require that the doula be certified. Some list specific training organizations, while others will establish a certain number of hours of training that must be completed. If you think you will work with clients using insurance benefits or Medicaid, it is very important to complete your certification. You may also want to pursue additional advanced trainings, such as ProDoula's Infant Feeding Educator, to ensure that you have sufficient learning to meet their requirements.

Another option that some clients might have for reimbursement is through their FSA or HSA benefits. If you are equipped to run credit card transactions for your business, then you will likely be able to process these payments. You may need to instruct your clients to check with their company's benefits manager to see if there are any specific details that should be included on the invoice to make sure that the support is covered.

A Website

In today's day and age, you NEED a website if clients are going to find you. If your budget allows, you can hire a professional web designer to build one for you. Otherwise, you can create your own website.

There are numerous DIY website platforms such as:

- Wordpress
- Squarespace
- Wix

All of these platforms offer easy-to-use templates to help you create a website with great SEO. ProDoula CEO, Randy Patterson, also offers affordable copywriting services to help you get your website published as quickly as possible

Your website does not have to be complex, however there are a few essential pages that you will want to consider including.

Homepage - Your Homepage is a potential client's first impression of your business. Since this can easily be the only page they visit before leaving, be sure to give a clear overall understanding of what you offer. This page should speak in your "brand's voice" and include an overview of your services, with links and language that encourage prospective clients to explore your website further. Be sure to have a call to action (link to contact you) on this page and all others.

About Page - Your About Page is where you can express your mission statement, share a statement of inclusivity and feature yourself and your expertise to prospective clients. This is the place to share more about yourself, what drew you to doula work, your training and experience, as well as some personal anecdotes.

Services Page - Your Services Page is where you will feature a more in depth description of the supportive services that you offer prospective clients. It is best to focus on the benefits of what you provide versus the features. Utilize language here that paints a picture of how your services can enhance the client's experience.

Contact Page - Your Contact Page is the place where prospective clients can inquire further about your services. Consider the information that you would like to know about this person and include it on the contact form. Keep in mind that requiring too much information before connecting with someone may deter them from contacting you at all. Keep it simple by asking for basic information such as:

- Name
- Phone number
- Email
- Due date

Blog Page - Your Blog Page is one of the best and most effective ways to increase your ranking in search engine results for doulas in your community. It is also a great opportunity to expose your community to the voice of your brand, your expertise, and further paint a picture of the type of support you offer and how it benefits your clients.

Get Doula Insurance

Although there is no legal structure from state to state regarding insurance for doulas, ProDoula strongly advises that you protect yourself and your assets with an insurance policy.

Currently, you are able to purchase doula insurance through CM&F Group Inc.

Contact them to apply for this very affordable coverage before beginning work as a doula.

Call the information center at CM&F: 800.221.4904 Or, visit them online for more information: *https://www.cmfgroup.com*

In Canada: LMS Prolink: *http://www.lmsprolink.ca/* or 800.663.6828

Create Contracts

Many business deals call for the creation of a written contract. A contract is a legal document that is designed to protect the parties involved from fraud and poor business practices. Hiring a lawyer to write or design a contract is often expensive and time consuming. Thus many people choose to write their own contracts. Contracts are recognized and used in a court system because they are considered legal documents. Therefore, you should always use care when you write a contract.

6 Tips For Writing Your Contract:

1. Word contracts simply and avoid unnecessary legal jargon.
2. List penalties and consequences if the agreement is not fulfilled.
3. Declare the monetary terms clearly.
4. Include the names, addresses, and telephone numbers for the contracting parties.
5. Clearly include the date of commencement in the contract.
6. Create an area for signatures and dates of all parties engaging in the contract.

Notes:

SAMPLE CONTRACT

Postpartum Support Contract

This Contract is between the parent/parents (hereinafter referred to as "Client"), and [Insert Doula's Name/Business Name] (hereinafter referred to as "Doula") for the purposes of providing postpartum doula support. After discussion and review, the parties agree as follows:

I. Services:

1. Doula has the necessary skills and training so as to enable Doula to perform the services for which the postpartum doula has been contracted for. Doula will support Client's decisions within the Doula's code of conduct.

2. The care provided by Doula includes, but is not limited to infant care, sibling care, infant feeding support, postpartum recovery support, errands, light housekeeping (e.g., laundry, washing bottles, loading dishwasher), and meal preparation. Doula will not provide any heavy housekeeping support, such as cleaning bathrooms, mopping, scooping litter boxes, etc.

3. Doula is not a medical provider and does NOT diagnose or treat medical conditions in the Client or baby, as this is outside Doula's code of conduct. Doula will also NOT administer medication to the Client or Client's baby as this is outside Doula's code of conduct.

4. Doula will NOT drive Client or Client's family either in Doula's car or Client's car.

5. Doula agrees to work with Client on a predetermined schedule, subject to availability and mutually agreeable hours. For billing purposes, an hour is considered to begin when Doula arrives at Client's home for the previously arranged shift.

6. If Doula works an overnight shift, Doula is permitted to sleep when the baby/babies is/are asleep, and all previously agreed upon duties have been completed.

7. When Doula is the adult in charge of a sleeping baby, Doula MUST follow the American Academy of Pediatrics Safe to Sleep Guidelines, which includes placing baby/babies on their back to sleep, in an approved, flat sleep surface.

8. Daytime shifts are a minimum of 5 hours and overnight shifts are a minimum of 10 hours. The latest time Doula can begin an overnight shift is 11:00 pm and the earliest an overnight shift can end is 6:00 am.

9. All contracted hours must be used within weeks [Insert contracted timeline] of date of commencement of services.

10. In the event Doula cannot provide postpartum support services as scheduled, due to unforeseen circumstances (i.e., family emergency, illness, weather), Doula will make all attempts to schedule a qualified, professional back-up doula to cover the shift or reschedule the postpartum services. Client shall be able to meet with back-up doula prior to this if Client chooses.

11. If Client wishes to extend the contract beyond the initial agreed-upon terms, Client understands that Doula will provide such services as staffing permits. Client and Doula will execute a new contract for services at that time.

II. Additional Provisions:

12. If the Client or any member of the Client's household is sick, including the baby, with fever, cough, vomiting, diarrhea, or any other contagious symptom, Client understands that Doula cannot work any agreed upon shifts during this time. Client will notify Doula at the onset of symptoms. Doula will resume support when the household is symptom free.

13. If Doula, or anyone in Doula's household, tests positive for Covid 19 or one of its variants, Doula will alert Client immediately. Services will be paused until Doula can provide a qualified, professional backup or until Doula provides proof of negative Covid test results, whichever the Client prefers.

14. If Client, or anyone in Client's household, tests positive for Covid 19 or one of its variants, Client will alert Doula immediately. Services will be paused until Client provides proof of negative Covid test results and Doula feels safe to return.

15. Client and Doula acknowledge the contagious nature of Covid 19 and its variants and understand that neither party can guarantee that the other party will not become infected, despite Client and Doula's best efforts

to prevent the spread of Covid. The parties understand that the risk of being exposed or becoming infected by Covid may result despite adhering to the highest safety guidelines.

Client Initials_____

III. Fee for Services:

16. Postpartum services will be provided at $_____ per hour [Insert hourly rate] with a minimum of _____ hours, [Insert minimum, if any] totaling $_____ . [Insert total for contract] A non-refundable retainer fee of $_____ [Insert retainer fee] is required at the signing of this contract. Client will be billed for all contracted hours except for the last_____ hours of care, [Insert hours covered by retainer fee] which will be satisfied by the retainer fee.

17. Doula will bill Client for postpartum services on a weekly basis. Payment must be made within 10 days of the posted date of billing. Failure by Client to timely pay will result in an additional charge equaling 5% of the bill amount.

18. If Client cancels a scheduled shift with less than 24 hours notice, Client will be billed for the requested, scheduled hours.

19. If the doula works for Client through an Agency, that doula is not for private hire. The hiring of a doula by Client, without the consent of the Agency, shall result in a $15,000.00 (fifteen thousand dollars) referral fee to be paid by Client to the Agency.

20. Client is responsible for any and all parking fees incurred at each shift. Parking fees will be included in the weekly billing.

21. We, the undersigned, have read this contract for postpartum doula services. We accept and agree to the terms and conditions.

Client Initials_____

Parent One (Printed Name) _____
Signature _____
Parent Two (Printed Name) _____
Signature _____
Address: _____

Phone Numbers: _____
Emails: _____
Due Date: _____
Birthing Facility: _____

_____
Doula

[Business Name]
[Address]
[Phone]
[Email]

Business Forms

There is no shortage of help on the Internet for people starting a new business. From business plans to profit and loss statements, most templates are available for free and are easy to download.

The truth is, that in order to start your business, you do not need complicated forms or software applications. For the first few years you will want to spend as much time as possible with clients or potential clients and as little time on the computer doing administrative work as you can.

The Client Intake Call

It is important to capture potential customer information when someone calls you and inquires about you or your business. During your intake call be sure to take notes regarding pertinent information.

The Art of the Intake Call

The intake call is often the doula's first chance to demonstrate what it is like to have the supportive care of a doula. The intention of this call is connection. Show the potential client through their interactions with you what it feels like to have you by their side, providing information and support from the start.

These calls will typically last between 30-40 minutes. During the call, focus on building a relationship with the individual on the other end of the phone. Be mindful and intentional about what experience you want the person to have during the call.

Tracking Form

It is important to track customers through each step of your business relationship with them. At times you may want to compare customer information or group the information by month, service type, etc. This is why we recommend that you use Excel, Google Sheets, or a similar program, to create a customer file that is easy to maintain.

Income Statement

An income statement, or profit and loss statement, is a financial statement that summarizes a company's revenues and business expenses to provide the big picture of its financial performance over several years.

Customer Relationship Management (CRM) Software

As your doula business grows, you may find it difficult to stay organized. Keeping track of intake forms, customer files, signed contracts, etc. is time consuming when done on a larger scale. Customer Relationship Management (CRM) software can help you manage client inquiries, create to-do lists for you and your team, keep track of client contracts and documents, organize business files, and more.

Some of the more popular CRM software for doula businesses include:

- Dubsado
- Basecamp
- 17 Hats

Investing in a good CRM software will allow your business to keep growing, while making it easier for you to manage all of its day-to-day business needs.

Marketing Your Doula Business

Once you have established your doula business, created a website, and organized all of the contracts and forms you will need, then it's time to find clients! In order for clients to find you, you have to market yourself. Marketing strategies can be divided between online - social media, blogging, email marketing campaigns, etc. - and in-person - meeting with providers, hosting events, warm chatting, etc. - marketing.

Marketing Tips

If It's Free, It's For Me!

- Utilize all of your free options first. Social networking is the wave of the future. Don't fight it! It is the most cost effective way to market and advertise a business.
- Network, Network, Network! Schedule your long overdue gynecologist appointment and let your doctor/midwife know of your new venture.
- Be sure to bring professional marketing materials with you and leave a great impression with the office staff. They are the ones who answer the phone when patients call for a doula referral!
- Join a committee that serves the birth world.
- A hospital maternity fair is a great start!
- Contribute to existing birth or postpartum related blogs.

Low Cost Marketing

- Become a Childbirth Educator or Infant Feeding Educator! Pregnant individuals may not be seeking the supportive services of a doula simply because they don't know what one is. But they do know what childbirth classes and other basic newborn care classes are! By becoming an educator through ProDoula, you will be seen as an expert and will have the opportunity to teach others about all of their options, including YOU as their doula!
- Marketing materials - business cards and rack cards can be printed inexpensively through Vistaprint or other online services.
- Offer to bring snacks to another birth professional's childbirth class or feeding class in exchange for the opportunity to do a short presentation about your services.
- Set up a lunch in a doctor's office to discuss the services that you provide (cost $60 - $100).
- Purchase a table at a birth related fair or show ($50 - $2,000).

Mid-High Range Budget

- Hire a professional web designer to build your website ($2,000 - $15,000).
- Hire a professional to shoot video or "commercials" to post on social media in order to drive traffic to your website ($500 - $5,000).
- Have your car wrapped with your company logo and design

- ($1,800 – $2,500).
- Rent or lease office space in a high visibility area ($300 - $3000 per month).

Consider participating in programs such as Carrot, state funded doula programs, or setting up your business to accept health saving or flexible spending accounts that allow potential clients to use these forms of insurance to partially or fully cover the expense of doula care. By doing so, you are creating the opportunity to market yourself in an additional way.

Streams of Income for Your Doula Business

The most obvious way to generate income as a doula is of course by providing doula services. As a labor doula or a postpartum doula, you will charge a flat rate or an hourly rate and you will be paid in direct proportion to how often you work. However, your earning potential is not limited to the number of hours you are available.

Consider these other options and allow yourself to explore others as your business grows.

Teach Childbirth Education, Newborn Care, and Infant Feeding Classes

Position yourself as the expert on all things related to birth and postpartum. As more clients enroll in your classes, more and more of them will also hire you to be their doula. Look into ProDoula's Childbirth Educator or Infant Feeding Educator Certifications, as well as ProDoula's curriculums for childbirth, newborn care, and infant feeding classes for sale in the ProDoula online shop.

Provide Placenta Services

Learning to provide placenta encapsulation services or hiring someone to do it can be financially rewarding and a valuable service for your clientele. For obvious reasons, always adhere to the highest standards when offering and providing these services.

Sell or Rent Products

Be sure to get a tax ID number and collect tax when applicable. Speak to your accountant about setting up the structure to accommodate this.

Growing Your Doula Business

As time goes on and as you take advantage of all the resources ProDoula has for you, your doula business will grow. Regardless of what business model is working for you, you might find yourself in the position to contract with other doulas to provide services.

As you develop name/brand recognition for your doula business more and more potential clients will be contacting you. You will be delighted to see the "fruit of your labor." However, by working independently, you will, at some point, reach the maximum number of clients appropriate to contract with for a given time period, and you will have to turn clients away or refer them to another doula.

Having worked hard to get your name out into the community it will be disappointing to refuse potential clients. Consider hiring other doulas as sub-contractors to work for you. In this scenario, a client hires your business and your business sets a standard of care that is modeled in your "team."

Pay your doulas a flat rate or an hourly rate and retain a portion of the fee for your efforts to acquire the clients, handle the scheduling of shifts, billing, and payroll. The ProDoula team is happy to offer you guidance if this is a direction you would like to grow in.

The Two Ways We Get Hired

Unlike labor doulas, who can only be hired prior to birth, postpartum doulas can be hired by clients either prenatally or after the baby arrives. A potential client reaching out during pregnancy is planning ahead. They may have a very ambiguous idea of what postpartum doula support looks like and you will need to paint an overall and helpful picture of what a postpartum doula does, especially if they have never experienced postpartum before. This client will likely want to interview you in person before making any final decisions about hiring.

On the other hand, a potential client that reaches out after their baby is born is in need of immediate help. During your intake call, ask very pointed questions about where they are struggling and where they need the most support and be sure to precisely explain how you can meet that exact need. This client may want to schedule a one-time "trial" shift with you before signing a larger package of postpartum hours. Once they experience the benefit of your support, they will want more and more.

The Interview

Part of growing your business must involve signing clients. Being confident and nailing the interview is essential.

The interview with the expectant parents may seem like a typical interview:

- You are meeting new people
- Selling yourself and your skills
- Getting the third degree about what you know or don't know

Yet during this type of interview you are trying to create a personal connection that will tell the client that you will be able to put them at ease at their most vulnerable time.

Things that let you know you are making a good connection during the interview:

- The client becomes more relaxed and comfortable
- The partner asks questions and engages in the conversation
- They start asking about your availability:
    - "What happens if the baby comes early?"

- "Can you meet us at home when we come home with our baby?"
  - "Can you provide overnight care?"
- YOU start feeling more of a connection to the parents.

Doula Consultation/Interview Tips:

Set an Intention – The goal is to have the parents choose YOU to be their doula! During the consultation, you will have the opportunity to paint a postpartum picture for the family - paint yourself into the picture.

Think About Your Ornaments – Clothes, make-up, and jewelry are all types of ornamentation that set you apart from others. Project an image that is professional, fun, and genuine. We all have some "power pieces" in our closets that make us feel our best. Plan on wearing those to your consultations.

List three "power pieces" in your wardrobe:

1)
2)
3)

Be Conscious of Your Body Language – Body language is a crucial part of first impressions. Often, being aware of your body language can result in immediate improvements. Consider videoing yourself with your phone as you practice answering interview questions.

Check Your Bad Day at the Door – When having a bad day, it is important to find a way to snap yourself out of your bad mood. On the way to the interview, turn on your favorite radio station, call your best friend, or treat yourself to your favorite Starbucks. Write an affirmation that you will "check" your mood before interacting with potential clients. Become known for always projecting great energy.

Be Interested and Engaging, It Is All About Them – When you are meeting for the first time, express a genuine interest in who they are. Ask open-ended questions that will help drive conversation and help you build rapport with potential clients.

Be On Time - On time means five to ten minutes early. If you are unfamiliar with the area, take some time to drive to the interview location ahead of time so you know exactly where you are going and how long it will take to get there.

Follow Up – Always follow up with potential clients.

Notes:

Goal Setting

When done properly, goal setting can be a very powerful tool. Unfortunately, without being taught how to set goals properly, many of us end up setting half-hearted goals and then feel terrible when we do not reach them.

Although goal setting has obvious value, we bring to each set of goals our feelings and thoughts about the last goal we set. If we succeeded at achieving our last goal, then we are filled with confidence as we tackle our next one. But if we failed at the previous goal or if we perceived it as a failure or feel that we have fallen short, then we will bring those feelings along with us as we begin working on the next goal.

CLEAR THE SLATE! Try it a different way. They say that if you always do what you always did, you'll always get what you always got. If we want something different, we must DO something different!

So, set a goal.

- Ask yourself, "WHAT do I want to accomplish?"
- And then ask yourself, "HOW will I accomplish it?

What is your strategy? You can't start with an "I'll figure it out" model. It must be deliberate. It might work for a short period, but success relies on a well thought out approach to "how."

You must believe you can do it. But it is likely you need some guidance and support. ProDoula is here to provide you with that!

www.ingramcontent.com/pod-product-compliance
Lightning Source LLC
LaVergne TN
LVHW061624070526
838199LV00070B/6567